RED FLAG

AIR COMBAT FOR THE '80S

RED FLAG

Michael Skinner
Photography by George Hall

THE PRESIDIO *AIRPOWER* SERIES

Presidio Press ★ Novato, California

Copyright ©1984 Michael Skinner

Photographs copyright ©1984 George Hall, with the following exceptions: p. 26, Michael Skinner collection; pp. 78–83, gun camera footage, courtesy 64th Aggressor Squadron; pp. 104–7, Bill Yenne; p. 122 right, Bill Yenne.

Published by Presidio Press, 31 Pamaron Way, Novato, CA 94947
Third printing 1986

Library of Congress Cataloging in Publication Data

Skinner, Michael, 1953–
   Red flag.

   1. Air warfare. 2. Fighter planes—United States.
3. War games. I. Hall, George (George N.) II. Title.
UG630.S5812   1984   358.4'156   83-13517
ISBN 0-89141-168-2

Design and Maps by Bill Yenne
Printed in the United States of America

Front cover
Left: A flight of 8th Tactical Fighter Squadron F–15s flies toward the fight over the Nellis range. *Right:* Four Aggressor F–5s in a variety of Warsaw Pact camouflage schemes over the Nevada desert. *Center:* The Aggressor's distinctive Red Flag insignia.

Back cover
Inside the Nellis control room during a Red Flag exercise.

Half-title page
An F–15 Eagle pilot climbs into the cockpit of his aircraft.

Title page
A brace of F–5 Aggressors maneuvers high over the parched badlands of the Great Basin.

Facing page
Pilots listen attentively to a pre-exercise briefing in the Red Flag meeting room.

Photographer's note: All photographs, except those noted above, were taken by George Hall with Nikon F3 and FE cameras, a variety of Nikkor lenses ranging from 15mm to 400mm, and Kodachrome-64 or Ilford FP 4 film.

Contents

Acknowledgments

Writing a book about Red Flag must be something like flying in Red Flag: there are a lot of things that have to be learned all at once. What George Hall and I have tried to do here is give the reader the *feeling* of flying in Red Flag, to show it through the eyes of the Players who go at each other five times a year over the Nevada desert. Red Flag is about the business of war in the air and how men are trained to fight it. We hope *Red Flag* is too. If the book works, it is largely thanks to these people:

Once again, here's to the indispensable Lt. Col. Eric Solander, head of the USAF's Books and Magazines Division in Washington. That's where it all starts. It all ends with Joan Griffin, our editor at Presidio Press, who has taught the author more about punctuation than he has taught her about airplanes.

In the middle, there's Nellis Air Force Base, which has perhaps the most professional public affairs shop we have had the pleasure of working with. The Tactical Fighter Weapons Center Public Affairs was run during our several visits by Lt. Col. David M. "Mike" Wallace, with a hand from Maj. Chris Weber. Lt. Liz Lane-Johnson served as our very own public affairs "Wild Weasel" at Nellis, clearing the way wherever we went, suppressing anything that stood in the way of our story.

We talked to dozens of pilots, backseaters, ground controllers, staff officers, ground crew, and innocent bystanders at the Tactical Fighter Weapons Center. We can't mention all of them, but here are the top dogs: Col. Joel "Tom T." Hall;

Fighter jocks return from afternoon of simulated combat over the Nellis range.

4440 TFTG (Red Flag); Lt. Col. Russ Everts, 64th Aggressor Squadron; Lt. Col. Mike Press, 65th Aggressor Squadron; Col. James T. "John" Glenn, DO of the Range Control Center; and all the Eagle drivers of the 49th TFW at Holloman AFB, New Mexico.

George Hall's air-to-air photographs of the 64th Aggressors and the 8th TFS "Black Sheep" Eagles were taken from the rear seat of an AT–38, with Capt. Al Phillips, 435th Tactical Fighter Training Squadron providing the driving, some excellent flight instruction, and even a bit of impromptu combat with the Players. George also hurtled over the Nellis range at 300 feet and less in the C–130s of the 37th TAS "Blue Tail Flies," Rhein-Main AB, Germany.

Thanks are due also to a bunch of civilians: in Nevada, Blake Morrison and Arkey Huber; and in Washington, Walt Boyne, Damian Houseman, and Bill Giltner.

Many sources were used in writing this book, but special mention must again be made of the USAF *Fighter Weapons Review (FWR)*; much of the Rules of Engagement (ROE) information was taken from Capt. Rich Hardy's excellent discussion on DACT ROE in the summer 1975 issue of *FWR*.

Since civilians are rarely allowed on actual Red Flag missions, the intent in Chapter 6 was to take the reader along on a typical one, reconstructed from interviews with pilots and tracked on the famous Big Board ("Blackjack") at Nellis. Although real enough in detail, some of the events may have happened on different missions, and in that sense the reconstructed mission is, to use the intel folks' favorite phrase, "completely notional."

Michael Skinner

Glossary

AAA: Antiaircraft Artillery

AAR: Air-to-Air Refueling

ACMI: Air Combat Maneuvering Instrumentation; a weapons range monitored by electronic beacons that receive signals from special pods carried by aircraft taking part in the exercise. The signals are processed through a computer, which displays the mock air battle on huge, four-color video screens that accurately portray the relative positions and flight parameters of all pod-equipped aircraft.

ADF: Air Defense Forces

AFFOR: Air Force Forces; "Blue" forces at Red Flag.

AIMVAL/ACEVAL: Air Intercept Missile Evaluation/Air Combat Evaluation; a series of operational tests conducted in the mid-seventies to determine the relative merits of competing USAF and Navy air-to-air missiles (AIMVAL) and later expanded to explore different theories of air combat (ACEVAL).

AWACS: Airborne Warning and Communications System; theoretically any sophisticated airborne radar aircraft, the term is used almost exclusively to refer to the Boeing E–3A Sentry.

AWC: Airborne Warning and Control

BAI: Battlefield Air Interdiction

BVR: Beyond Visual Range

CAP: Combat Air Patrol; usually combined with a prefix to denote a type of air combat mission— LOWCAP (low altitude fighter operations), RESCAP (protecting orbiting rescue helicopters and aircraft), and so on.

CAS: Close Air Support

CFB: Canadian Forces Base

CO: Commanding Officer

DACT: Dissimilar Air Combat Training

DO: Director of Operations

DSP: Defensive Suppression

ECM: Electronic Countermeasures; the use of special equipment to defeat or lessen the effectiveness of enemy guidance and fire-control systems.

ESA: Escort

FAA: Federal Aviation Administration

FAC: Forward Air Control

FAST: Fleet Air Superiority Training

FEBA: Forward Edge of Battle Area; in popular terms, the battlefield, or the front.

FLOT: Forward Line of Troops

FWR: Fighter Weapons Review

FWW: Fighter Weapons Wing

GCI: Ground Control Intercept

HUD: Head-Up Display; a clear video screen installed above the forward instrument panel in most modern aircraft displaying computer-generated navigation and weapons system information.

IFF: Identification, Friend or Foe; electronic devices designed to determine which unidentified aircraft are friendly and which are enemies.

ILS: Instrument Landing System

INT: Interdiction

MAC: Military Airlift Command

MiG: Mikoyan-Gurevich

MOA: Military Operating Area

NORDO: No Radio

OCA: Offensive Counter-Air

OPFOR: Opposition Forces; "Red" forces at Red Flag.

PACAF: Pacific Air Forces

RAF: Royal Air Force

REC: Reconnaissance

Wild Weasel electronics pods aboard an F–4G.

RHAW: Radar Honing and Warning
RIO: Radar Intercept Officer
ROE: Rules of Engagement
SAC: Strategic Air Command
SAM: Surface-to-Air Missile
SRAAM: Short Range Air-to-Air Missile
TAC: Tactical Air Command
TAF: Tactical Air Forces
TDY: Temporary Duty
TFTAS: Tactical Fighter Training Aggressor Squadron

TFTG: Tactical Fighter Training Group
TFWC: Tactical Fighter Weapons Center
TRS: Tactical Resupply
USAF: United States Air Force
USAFE: United States Air Forces in Europe
VFR: Visual Flight Rules
VPAAF: Vietnam People's Army Air Forces

Chapter 1
Student Gap

North of the neon furnaces and gambling pits of Las Vegas is a bigger game played for higher stakes. In this strange game there is no score, but there are winners and losers. The winners win nothing but the chance to play again; the losers lose everything. The game is called Red Flag, and it is strictly for the highest rollers of all.

If you head north out of Vegas, past the sprawling Nellis Air Force Base, past where the highway curves prudently east, away from the U.S. Air Force's live bombing ranges, you will come to a cut between two, hard brown mountains. Earthlings call this pass, where State Highway 93 intersects the 115th meridian, the Pahroc Summit. But it has another name.

If you leave your air conditioning and scramble out among the creosote and the blackbrush, you will soon wish you hadn't. The heat will assault you, the glare will blind you, but it is the desolation, the sheer aloneness of the place, that will drive you to the edge. There is no sound, no sound at all, save for the occasional humming of an automobile sensibly leaving the middle of nowhere.

But if you stay out here long enough, something will happen. You will feel it long before you see it — a vague premonition, a sense of thunder from the

A comprehensive mix of modern tactical aircraft line the ramp at Nellis Air Force Base. Downtown Las Vegas is in the distance.

east. If it is one of those quartz-clear days that are not uncommon in this part of the country, you might even see it coming: a black dot hovering over the shimmer of the highway as it runs east to the little town of Caliente.

Immediately the dot swells and sprouts wings. It is upon you in an instant, a smoking, hulking beast scorching across the desert at 500 miles per hour. Before your mind can categorize and dismiss it (it is, after all, only an Air Force F–111 fighter bomber), there is an initial sense of awe and terror. With its pivoting wings swept back, the aircraft resembles an ancient pterodactyl, the huge, leather-winged monster that haunted this desert in prehistoric times. When that enormous shadow falls across you, it is easy to feel the ancient flight-or-fight impulse of the caveman. The feeling clutches at your throat and holds you in its dark power. That moment is gone in a heartbeat, but the memory will never leave.

As quickly as it appeared, the plane is gone. The pterodactyl's shadow scuttles over the brown scrub and folds itself up Mount Irish. The radar in its long black snout nods and swivels in its gimbals, searching for the rocks and mountains in its path. The F–111 shoots the pass low and fast, barely a hundred feet above the desert.

Like the sidewinder, another citizen of the desert floor, for every F–111 you see, there are dozens of planes you don't. High above your head, up where the sky curves into indigo, is a constant parade of airpower over the Pahroc Summit. Just

about every kind of aircraft from every branch of the free world's flying services has overflown that coordinate. They call it Student Gap. It's where the game begins, where the players cross the in-bounds marker, Checkpoint Charlie, on the way to Redland. It's the start of the Red Flag world, and the closest you or I will get to the Big Game.

From here on, the pilots are on their own, fair game for the false MiGs and fake antiaircraft gun and missile batteries that lie in wait for the unprepared. When they push the Gap, the pilots are as close to war as anyone would want to get. Some careless or unlucky pilots will "die." Some truly careless or tragically unlucky pilots could die for . real, as others have before. There are strict safety rules, but no rules can remove completely the

Aggressor pilots head for their F–5s on the Red Flag ramp.

danger involved in high-Mach jousting, in aircraft buzzing around one another like supersonic dragonflies, in dragging live bombs so low their shadows are tucked underneath them.

This inherent danger is what Red Flag is all about—an introduction to life at the edge for the young tigers. Red Flag may not be a precise simulation of the next war. How can it be? But the *pressure* of war is there—nothing simulated about that.

"There's a tremendous amount of pressure here," says a pilot taking part in Red Flag for the first time. "You sense it when you walk in the door. Everybody's under the gun."

"It's a learning situation," says an F-15 pilot. "You can't always back off. There's going to be times when you're thrust into a situation and they say, 'Hey, react!'"

"If you compare Red Flag with war, then yes, the level of violence here is much, much lower," says a Red Flag staff officer. "But for the guy who's never been to combat—when he comes to Red Flag he is a very, very busy young man."

That's what Red Flag is all about, to give the young fighter pilot combat experience in the absence of combat. Maybe you can't build an exact replica of the air defenses of a Soviet Motorized Rifle Division in the Nevada desert; but you *can* simulate the disorientation of combat, the sensory overload that is often more dangerous to inexperienced pilots in combat than all the guns, SAMs and MiGs ever built. To the young tigers who *think* they have the juice, Red Flag gives new meaning to the term "pressurized cockpit."

Red Flag is often called a game, but it is more like a sport, where teamwork and timing count more than mere athletic ability. It is event-oriented training, a problem with as many solutions as there are participants. It is not an inspection or an evaluation. It is not a test, but rather a place to be tested, an opportunity for new pilots to make their first mistakes and for veterans to try something new in a realistic environment without getting killed. It is a place for the men who operate the U.S. Air Force's diverse, but increasingly interdependent, weapons systems to meet, argue, laugh, think, and train with one another. Most important, it is a chance for warriors to get wartime experience without risk.

"We do not evaluate people at Red Flag. We don't test people, we don't give them check rides, and we don't let the wings have Operational Readiness Inspections at Red Flag. No evaluations," says the Red Flag CO. "It's a learning program, and we don't want them put under the pressure of a test or evaluation because, invariably, people who are being tested do not learn. It's like a golfer

choosing between the high-percentage shot as opposed to the one that he *thinks* he might be able to pull off. So we want people to *train* here, not go back to the high-percentage shot."

Like the rest of the Air Force's newer training programs, Red Flag is the result of the USAF's poor showing in the war in Southeast Asia. One of the few good things that came from that bad war was the rediscovery of some old rules of air combat, rules the United States had long forgotten and had to relearn the hard way over Route Pack 6.

Most pertinent to Red Flag was the axiom that a pilot's chances for survival, as well as his effectiveness, rises dramatically in relation to the number of combat missions he flies. It doesn't take many missions—ten seems to be the optimum number; after that, diminishing returns set in, and the pilot is probably as good as he is going to get.

The problem was providing inexperienced pilots with ten combat missions' worth of experience without exposing them to actual combat. The Air Force's post-Vietnam emphasis on realistic training programs had already produced a simulated enemy force, the Aggressors, and a realistic battlefield, complete with threats and targets, on the Nellis AFB range. What was needed was a way to tie it all together, to use those assets to give young USAF pilots a head start in air combat. The solution was Red Flag, and the man with the plan was Richard M. "Moody" Suter.

"Moody is today, and was then, the kind of guy who aggressively pursues what everybody knows to be good ideas," the current Red Flag CO says of the program's founder, now a USAFE staff colonel.

They were not, by any stretch of the imagination, ideas unique to Moody Suter. But what he did was travel the world and, literally, take notes at the bar; he'd write them down on bar napkins. As he would visit air bases, both during and after the Southeast Asia war, he compiled a long list of ideas from people he talked to. And there was one common

thread: We didn't go far enough in our training programs to prepare for war. And that discontinuity between what we did in peacetime and wartime was costly.

It was not that USAF training was bad; it just didn't go far enough. It took pilots right up to the point of realistic air combat training and left them hanging there. Even worse, after initial training, pilots were relegated to "flying around the flag-pole," concerned only with logging the required number of flight hours, not what those missions consisted of. During a period in the 1960s, one "fighter" squadron in England did not fly a single air-to-air training mission for three years. Their experience was not unique. When you have multi-role aircraft, such as the F–4 and the F–105, the

Above and right: A Seymour-Johnson AFB F-4 crew starts engines for an afternoon Red Flag "go."

USAF's workhorses in Vietnam, you need multi-role pilots, and if the line jocks are required to be proficient in everything from dogfights to dropping the Big One, there's barely enough time to stay current and precious little time to become good at anything.

"We set out, in '75, and we looked at tactical fighter training across the board to find out what was missing," says the Red Flag CO.

The answer, really, was that there wasn't anything missing; it just did not go far enough. We stopped at too low a proficiency level, in terms of

the broad, dynamic types of decisions that you would have to make in combat. We were stopping far too short.

So we set out, then, to structure a flying training program that didn't fundamentally change what we had done in the past, but added an extension to it, to go from undergraduate level to graduate or doctorate level.

Moody Suter not only listened, he talked, and eventually he got the ear of Gen. Robert J. Dixon, then commander of the Tactical Air Command. General Dixon knew a good idea when he heard one. (He was later awarded the Collier Trophy for establishing Red Flag.) Within a very short period of time, three or four months, the first Red Flag was held at Nellis AFB in November 1975.

That was almost ten years ago, but Red Flag 75-1 was almost identical in concept to contemporary Red Flags, showing how right the idea was. Every Red Flag exercise then, as now, follows this typical pattern:

—A scenario is written by the Red Flag intelligence people concerning the imminent hostilities between "Red," the "bad guys" who live on the western side of the Nellis range, and "Blue," the allies, defending the neighboring eastern part of the range.

—Most Red Flag exercises last six weeks, but the "Players," the Red Flag participants, are rotated every two weeks, so the war effectively lasts only ten days with no flying taking place on the weekend. Each Player flies ten missions, the

first mission always a familiarization ride orienting the new Player to the Nellis range.

—The Blue Forces consist of the "core unit" and detachments from other units. The Red Forces consist of F–5Es from the 64th and 65th Aggressor Squadrons at Nellis, as well as detachments from other air units and the simulated SAM and Antiaircraft artillery (AAA) batteries out on the range.

—Each mission is coordinated by a different "warlord." Before and after each mission there is a mass briefing of all participating Players, as well as individual briefings among the flights

F-4s and an aging F-105 Thunderchief on the ramp.

and even face-to-face debriefings with the Red Players.

Red Flag is not a no-notice deployment drill. The Players can know a year and a half ahead that they're scheduled to come to Red Flag. A surprise invitation to come to Nellis wouldn't serve any real purpose other than to embarrass the grossly unprepared. That would violate one of the unwritten rules of Red Flag, which is to take advantage of every action, every deployment, and learn something from it.

"There are two elements of combat," says a Red Flag officer.

Getting there, for the United States, is half the problem. Fighting when you get there is going to get the publicity, but the fundamental issue is that you must be able to get there. So there is a small but very important part of Red Flag dedicated to the deployment phase.

Before they [the players] *come to Red Flag, they've got to make sure any minor* [maintenance] *write-up is fixed, and all the time-change maintenance requirements are taken care of on their aircraft. When they're loading up the cargo planes, they've literally got to put max gross weight on every aircraft and no cubic feet wasted. We also process the people as if they were going to war. There's no difference, as far as the processing goes—the shots and the paperwork—whether they're turning left and going to Nellis or turning right and going to Europe.*

Even the pilots are not immune to the rigors of mock deployment. Used to leisurely stopovers on their way cross-country, Red Flag players are obliged to make the trip to Nellis all at once, following a tanker for eight hours at a stretch. "We want it to hurt as much as possible," says the Red Flag CO, "because it's going to hurt when you have to turn around and go the other direction for ten or twelve hours.

Red Flag is run by the Tactical Air Command (TAC), but units from every branch of the Air Force, the other U.S. flying services, and various Allies participate in the program. ("The first exercise was TAC," says a Nellis veteran. "It changed fast after that.") But one thing never changes: The "core unit" will always be a front-line TAC fighter wing. Since fighter wings usually consist of three squadrons, Red Flag is most often split into three two-week periods, and units from each of the wing's three squadrons deploy in turn.

"I'll normally have anywhere from seventeen to twenty different units at each exercise," says the Red Flag CO. "But I can't bring seventeen different squadrons in here. I don't have the ramp space; I don't have the help. So only one of those units will be a full squadron, from squadron commander down to the lowest maintenance and support guy. That's the fighting unit—they all wear the same hat. That 'core unit' will be the fundamental character driver of that exercise."

"Character driver" means that the "core unit," because of sheer numbers, will exert the most powerful influence on how the scenario is written and how the missions are structured. For example, if the core unit is an A-10 outfit, expect the enemy to have a lot of tanks and our allies to need help along the Forward Edge of Battle Area (FEBA). Or if the core unit flies Eagles, look for a lot of air-to-air action.

But the other Players have an input as well. Here's how the Red Flag commander looks at it:

Six weeks prior to each exercise, I start looking at each unit, finding out the level of their individual training programs and where they want to start the war, in terms of difficulty. Because there's such a broad variety of wartime capability represented, each one has to be worked into the war. In other words, if I have rescue coming, I've got to have somebody shot down.

You have a pretty stabilized mix of aircraft at Red Flag: reconnaissance and rescue people, airlift, AWACS, strategic bombers, choppers, as well as lots of air-to-air fighters, lots of air-to-ground fighters, and the close air support. So there's one fairly steady characteristic about Red Flag: it looks like our force posture."

There are usually five Red Flag exercises each year. As of mid-1983, a total of 26,800 crewmembers had flown 228,275 hours in 134,694 Red Flag sorties. Each Red Flag is designated by the year and the number of exercises held up to that one; for example, "Red Flag 83-5" would be the fifth Red Flag exercise held in 1983 (or as the Players say, "World War 83-5").

7

Left: Ordnance loading at Nellis usually takes place in the cooler after-dark hours. *Above:* F-4 crew joins takeoff lineup. Phantoms lack air conditioning, unlike newer "teen generation" fighters.

There are also a couple of Maple Flag exercises held annually, in conjunction with the Canadian Armed Forces. Maple Flag and Red Flag are almost identical in theme and content, the big difference being the environment. Maple Flag is held at CFB (Canadian Forces Base) Cold Lake, Alberta, 180 miles northeast of the provincial capital, Edmonton, and miles and miles from anything else. Its Air Combat Maneuvering Range comprises 4,630 square miles, from 3,000 feet up. There is also a tactical target range 110 miles long and 40 miles wide, with simulated SAMs, AAA, airfields, etc. But

the biggest benefit to the USAF, according to one Aggressor pilot, is the scenery:

Nellis does not even approximate Europe, and most of the U.S. air-to-ground aircraft are camouflaged for a green environment. Put those green airplanes over a light-colored desert out here, and it's much easier for them to be seen. Maple Flag is a lot better for the camouflage—there's lots of greenery up there, and it's a lot harder to find people.

"You can only simulate what the atmosphere around here allows you to simulate," says another Aggressor.

The Nellis range space up here is probably the world's greatest for simulating the battle over the Mideast; it's almost identical, except it's probably not quite as hot. It's certainly not the same as Europe, and that's primarily why they've got Maple

9

Flag. I spent four years flying F-4s out of Bitburg [West Germany], and the Maple Flag environment is excellent for simulating the European theater: the weather's crummy, there's lots of green trees on the ground, and it's hard to figure out where you are.

A Navy F-4 of VF-202 passes Holloman AFB F-15s as it taxis in from a Red Flag flight.

Another Red Flag "clone" is the Pacific Air Force's Cope Thunder program. Like Red Flag and Maple Flag, Cope Thunder's main purpose is to give the young fighter pilot ten missions' worth of combat experience. The first Cope Thunder exercise was held in mid-1976, making it almost as old as Red Flag itself. Cope Thunder is held twice a year at Clark Air Base, in the Philippines, sixty miles northeast of Manila on the island of Luzon. Clark AB is the largest American military instal-

lation outside the United States (although, under the new treaty, Clark is now technically a United States reservation on a Philippine government base, and the new base commander is a Filipino).

The Cope Thunder missions take place over the Crow Valley Tactical Electronic Warfare Range, with its "Realistic Target Area"—the inevitable simulated SAMs, AAA, tanks and airfields—and "Conventional Target Area," with its scorable bomb range and acoustically scored strafe targets.

USAFE, the other member of the TAF (tactical air forces), doesn't have a Red Flag–type program. They have the Aggressors, they have some simu-

An F/A-18 of VMFA-314 (Marines) sports a dummy AIM-9 Sidewinder air-to-air missile.

lated target ranges, and they even have a vast Air Combat Maneuvering Range at Decimommannu on Sardinia, but no room to put them all together. Their biggest exercise is Cold Fire, the tactical air segment of the annual Reforger exercises; but Cold Fire is more of a traditional war game than Red Flag.

The U.S. Navy's Top Gun program has often been compared to Red Flag and the Aggressors, but it is not quite like either of them. For one thing, Top Gun is older. Its origins go back to 1969, when VF-121, the Pacific Fleet replacement training squadron, initiated "The U.S. Navy Postgraduate Course in Fighter Weapons, Tactics and Doctrine," an intensive air-to-air training program for the USN F-4 community. (The name, which took

longer to say than most dogfights, was quickly shortened to "Top Gun," even though Navy Phantoms didn't carry guns.) Top Gun came about as the result of the U.S. Naval Air Systems Command's now-famous "Ault Report" (officially titled the "Air-to-Air System Capability Review of 1968"), a study of the reasons for the U.S. Navy's poor showing in dogfights over North Vietnam. The study was directed by Capt. Frank W. Ault, an ex-skipper of the carrier U.S.S. Coral Sea.

Before Top Gun, the Navy's kill ratio was about the same as the Air Force's—from two- or three-to-one. The reasons for the poor records of both

Marine F/A-18 refuels from its KC-130 tanker en route to Red Flag.

services were also similar: inferior missile performance, restrictive rules of engagement, and, most of all, poor training for dogfighting. Although both services were using brand-new F-4s with their long-range radar missiles which were supposed to eliminate it, dogfighting was still a reality of air combat.

Top Gun became an independent command in 1972, chartered as the U.S. Navy Fighter Weapons School. Top Gun was extremely effective in training Navy fighter jocks for air-to-air combat. For the Navy, the air-to-air scorecard over Southeast Asia could be split into two segments: before Top Gun—2:1, and after Top Gun—13:1. The Air Force's kill ratio, however, remained relatively constant, and it is safe to assume the Top Gun program had some influence in the realistic training programs the USAF came up with toward the end of the war in Vietnam.

But Top Gun is not like Red Flag. It is strictly air-to-air. (A separate course, Fleet Air Superiority

Training [FAST], teaches Marine Air Superiority which is mostly electronic warfare training for F-14 RIOs [Radar Intercept Officers] and ship-based and E-2C GCI [Ground Control Intercept] controllers, concerned with protecting the carrier task forces with ultra-long-range missiles.) Only in the last stages of the program do Top Gun students drill with large numbers of other types of aircraft, simulating an Alpha Strike. Neither do the Top Gun instructors simulate Soviet tactics to the degree done by the USAF Aggressors—mostly they just fly the best F-5 or A-4 they can. "I think Top Gun tries to teach you how to beat the best Russian pilot that ever lived," says a Naval Reserve F-4 jock at Red Flag. "They're that good." Top Gun is more like the USAF Fighter Weapons School, an extensive course on air-to-air tactics given to selected students who, in turn, go back to their squadrons and share what they've learned.

Marine pilots regularly attend Top Gun, but because of their specialized mission, Marine Corps pilots also have a separate postgraduate training program, Marine Aviation and Tactics Squadron One's Weapons and Tactics Instructor Course, a seven-week advanced flying and academic exercise dealing exclusively with ground support. The students' "final exam" is an exercise called "FINEX" which may involve up to seventy aircraft, at the range adjoining Marine Corps Air Station, Yuma, Arizona, not too far south of Nellis and Red Flag.

But no other nation stages realistic training exercises on anything like the level or intensity of Red Flag. And that includes the Soviet Union.

"We've seen in Warsaw Pact training some multi-ship-type attacks and 'we'll attempt to defend' kinds of scenarios," says an Aggressor pilot. "But I don't think it's run at the rate Red Flag is."

Probably the main reason there is no real *Red Red Flag* is that the Soviets don't need it. Not because they're that good—their training could certainly stand some improvement—but the type of training Red Flag tries to provide would be wasted on the average Soviet pilot. Why teach him to think for himself in an exercise, when real life Soviet tactics strive to breed the individuality out of every MiG jock and make him into part of a rigid machine?

"Once a year, in some of their big exercises, they'll mess a bunch of airplanes around," says an Aggressor CO.

But the way their system is designed, with a lot of control, a lot of regimentation in it, it's not an easy thing to change. Yeah, they're doing a little more experimenting with some of their more senior aviators, particularly some of their Flogger things because it's got more capability on its own than the MiG–21 does.

"After all," chuckles a Red Flag officer, "every time they train initiative into one of their pilots, he flies his Foxbat to Japan."

Other nations don't even go as far as the Soviets do in realistic training.

"Certainly not any of the Soviet Bloc, Soviet allied countries, third world countries that have their own little air forces—the Syrians, for example—train anywhere near like what we do," says an Aggressor CO. "That, I think, becomes very obvious when you look at the Middle East, the successes the Israelis have had."

"In an air force such as Syria, where you have 600–700 jet-qualified pilots, you'll have 15 or 20 exceptionally gifted, qualified, knowledgeable aviators and you'll have about 580 hamburgers," says another Aggressor pilot. "Some of their pilots are, apparently, very poor, and they genuinely hate their Russian advisors. The Russian technique of training is 'You *will* do it this way!' And, of course, they think a lot differently. So they don't learn very much from their advisors."

But some American allies have the same problem. Almost every American ally has been to Red Flag, and most do very well. But the Players from some of the less-developed nations often have a tough time adjusting. They are given language lessons before they come to Nellis, and some are even given check-rides over the range (the only exception to the "no-check-rides" rule at Red Flag). But nothing in their training program can prepare them for the intensity they find at Red Flag. It is air-to-air culture-shock for some foreign pilots.

"Different countries have different personalities. You don't debrief foreign pilots the way you debrief your own people," says an Aggressor pilot.

I think the Brits and the French understand because they have their own exercises and they take their flying seriously. They're Westernized nations; when they were little kids there were cars running around. The Saudis were here, the Jordanians were here. The Thais, in particular, were

overwhelmed—there were jets on the left, jets on the right, everybody going a thousand miles an hour—strictly overwhelmed.

As the Red Flag commander puts it:

There is always a sensitivity with foreign participants. As you know, it depends on the time of day and perhaps the day of the week whether or not you're getting along with one of your friends, or whether you've got a beef with one of your friends. We do not go full U.S. Top Secret out here and spill our guts to anybody. There are certain things we just don't do in exercises and certainly don't talk about in the building and briefing rooms when there are foreign participants.

Sometimes America's changing relations with other countries can be an ironic blessing. According to a Red Flag Officer:

For the Red Team: Aggressor F–5Es in varied Warsaw Pact camouflage schemes and large nose numbers.

When we bring in the U.S. Army's Hawk batteries, we can play them on the Red side or the Blue side. Because you never know these days— we've sold those things to everybody.

A lot of people, including many aviation writers, have the wrong idea about Red Flag. The Aggressors hear it all the time:

"Probably the largest misconception is that people think *we're* Red Flag, and we're not," says a frustrated 64th Aggressor Squadron Pilot.

We only augment Red Flag. We support them as we do anybody else. Our main job is to get out into

the field around TAC and fly against those units. We fly with Red Flag only as support.

Technically, Red Flag is no more than the 4440th Tactical Fighter Training Group, just a dozen or so rated officers and their enlisted help pushing papers around Building 201. But Red Flag is supported by the Aggressors, the range group, and lots of other organizations around Nellis, all part of the Tactical Fighter Weapons Center. The TFWC is a very interesting organization, whose component parts support, and are supported by, the other parts. The whole thing is like a box full of coat hangers. It's probably best to start at the beginning.

The TFWC, founded in 1966, is currently divided into three parts—the headquarters, support, and operations branches.

Head Aggressor Col. Hugh Moreland lets fly with the traditional gomer go-sign as he taxis for takeoff.

HQ TFWC is home for the commander, the vice commander, the command section, and the chief of staff for programs and resources. The latter heads the special staff, with deputies that oversee such operations as plans, public affairs, administration, safety, the communications-electronics staff officer, the chief of air traffic and aerospace coordination, and even the chief of protocol.

The 554th Operations Support Wing, responsible for TFWC support, is divided into six sections. Probably the most important, from the Red Flag point of view, is the 554th Range Group, charged

with maintaining and operating the vast bombing ranges north of Nellis. There is also the 554th Combat Support Squadron, which performs most of the routine "housekeeping" functions at Nellis —Security Police, personnel and so on. There are two deputates: the 554th Deputy Commander for Resource Management, handling supply, logistics, and transportation for the TFWC; and the Deputy Commander for Civil Engineering, who builds and maintains any sort of specialized construction projects for the TFWC, both at Nellis and out on the range. The other two 554th OSW units are the U.S. Air Force Hospital at Nellis and Social Actions, an organization charged with administering the Air Force's "People Programs" at Nellis—drug and

Above: Colonel Moreland and wingman rotate against Sunrise Mountain backdrop. *Right:* Navy and Air Force Phantoms jam the Nellis ramp during Red Flag 82–5.

alcohol abuse control and treatment, equal opportunity, and human relations education.

The third component of the TFWC is the 57th Fighter Weapons Wing, in charge of all the TFWC's flying operations. This is a rather unique outfit and gets its share of publicity, which is understandable considering its famous subunits:

—The U.S. Air Demonstration Squadron: The Thunderbirds, now zooming around in new tutti-frutti F–16 Electric Jets, are familiar sights at Nellis.

An EF-111A "Spark 'Vark" tactical jamming aircraft.

—The Adversary Tactics Directorate: The parent unit of Nellis' two Aggressor Squadrons, the 64th and 65th AS, it also conducts the training programs for new Aggressor pilots and radar operators.

—4513th Adversary Threat Training Group: The "master intelligence unit" of the 57th FWW and the TWFC is charged with gathering military-related information from a variety of intelligence sources. In terms of tactics and briefing information, the Aggressors get most of their up-to-date information on what the other side is doing from the 4513th, who also have a lot of input into Red Flag scenario generation.

—The U.S. Air Force Fighter Weapons School: This is the nearest USAF equivalent to the Navy's Top Gun program, where selected TAC A-10, F-4, F-15, F-16, and F-111 line pilots receive a postgraduate course in their particular aircraft. The FWS graduates return to their squadron to teach what they've learned at Nellis to the other pilots.

—Deputy Commander for Tactics and Testing: This deputate is responsible for TAC "OT & E," the operational test and evaluations of different weapons systems and tactics. The tests are conducted by three Test and Evaluation Squadrons sharing the same "WA" tail-coded aircraft with the FWS. Two of the squadrons are at Nellis: the 422nd TES, flying the A-10, F-4, F-15, and F-16; and the 4477th TES, flying the F-5E and T-38. The other squadron, the 431st TES, flies F-111s out of McClellan AFB, California.

—4440th Tactical Fighter Training Group (Red Flag): On paper, Red Flag looks puny—no aircraft of its own, no ranges, few personnel. Red Flag ties a lot of the TFWC together in a single exercise; so

The Red Flag ramp. A Hill AFB F-105 "Thud" is at left.

when there's a Red Flag going on, the 4440th TFTG commander has operational control of a tremendous number of resources.

This isn't all the TFWC does, and by no means everything located at Nellis. There is, for example, an F–16 outfit, the 474th TFW, stationed on the base. It's hard to lose something like an entire fighter wing, but Nellis has a way of swallowing things up.

"It's the only fighter base in the world where the Thunderbirds could just get lost," says a Nellis officer. "There's just so much going on."

Nellis is a big base, but no base is big enough for fighter pilots' egos. Sometimes it seems as if the units wish the others would go away and stop stealing their thunder. But there's a more significant reason for tension between the units than mere jealousy. Nellis may be a big base, with a big range, but everybody has to take off and land on the same two runways. And those runways, crowded enough with the regular 57th FWW activities, get choked up when sixty-odd visitors fly in for Red Flag. It's starting to become a problem.

"The thing I was impressed by was the lack of priority that Red Flag has at Nellis," says a Navy Phantom jock playing on the Red side.

Red Flag is just a small part of this place— they've got the Aggressors, the Fighter Weapons School, and everything else. And part of the problem—and it is a problem—is that they can have situations, which we've already seen, where they get all of the Blue Force off, and the Red Force is stuck on the ground because of all the landing and take-off traffic. And by the time they [the Red Force] get out there, the strikers have already come in and blown everything away.

Left: Ground crewmen await chief's signal to pull wheel chocks on a Moody AFB Phantom. *Above:* Aggressor F-5 heads for the Nellis range.

But if the Blue Force gets hung up at the end of the runway, it's just as bad, as this Aggressor pilot explains:

Because Red Flag tries to group the airplanes in a large group force trying to attack the targets and go air-to-air, if we're not there at the right time, we'll spend some time loitering. And because of the distance we have to fly out there, we're usually limited to fifteen or twenty minutes maximum on station.

For the Red Flag Players, the most frustrating part of the mission is not bombing difficult targets or hassling it out air-to-air—they *enjoy* that—but just getting the force out of Nellis together. Red Flag missions are constantly marred by people taking off late, through no fault of their own, and spoiling the flight for both sides.

There is also a growing demand on range space at Nellis. It's huge, all right, but so are the demands upon it, not just by Red Flag but by all the other 57th FWW operations. "We've got 35 percent more customers than we can handle now," says a range group officer, and the demand is increasing every year. The TFWC has its hands full trying to avoid a full-fledged range war north of Nellis.

Probably the most famous 57th FWW units are Nellis' two Aggressor squadrons, who mimic Soviet tactics in their uniquely camouflaged F-5Es. Although, as has been pointed out, the Aggressors are *not* Red Flag, they are in every exercise and are the premier "character driver" of the Red forces. Let's take a closer look at the Aggressors.

21

Chapter 2
Meet the Aggressors

You might say the U.S. Air Force's greatest instructor pilot was a North Vietnamese MiG jockey, Nguyen Van Bay. Although he shot down thirteen American planes to become the leading ace of the war on either side, the Aggressors speak of Van Bay with respect, if not . . . gratitude. After all, he managed to do what countless USAF majors, colonels, and even generals couldn't: he got the U.S. Air Force into the realistic air-to-air training business.

Nguyen Van Bay was born in 1936, in the south of what was then French Indochina. As a teenager, he fought with the Vietminh against the French, and when the country was partitioned in 1954 he stayed in the north, growing rice. In 1961 he was tapped for pilot training by the Soviets, who were helping to organize the Vietnam People's Army Air Force (VPAAF).

Like many aces, Van Bay had a rough time in primary training. In his first few flights he got airsick, but his stomach eventually settled down, and he checked out in the MiG–17. He was assigned to Capt. Ho Van's 2nd Company, a Fresco fighter squadron based outside Hanoi.

Although details of his kills are often contradictory, it is generally conceded that Van Bay shot down about seven American pilots in the early years of the war. He took advantage of the bomb-ing halt between 1968 and 1972 to go back to Soviet Russia and transition to the MiG–21C. When the American airstrikes resumed with the Linebacker operations, Van Bay returned to the skies of Route Pack 6A to shoot down six more U.S. aircraft.

The fact that more than a dozen of their aircraft were shot down by the same pilot bugged the USAF, but that wasn't the point; after all, the infamous North Vietnamese ace, Colonel Tomb, allegedly shot down just as many. (That is, if Tomb actually existed—the North Vietnamese, always anxious to publicize the exploits of their Hero Air Force, are curiously mum when it comes to Tomb.) But the important thing about Van Bay, from the Air Force point of view, is that he *survived*. Tomb was shot down by U.S. Navy ace Randy Cunningham.

The air war over North Vietnam was a crazy part of a crazy war, and it would have been easy to dismiss the Air Force's poor showing as a factor of the frustrating restrictions under which they were forced to fight. But many USAF pilots felt the causes went even deeper, to the training and tactics of American fliers, and Red Baron proved them correct.

The Red Baron study was put together while the war was still going on. An interim report was released in 1972, but the complete study—volumes of it, all still classified—was distributed in 1974. If the whole project was an immense undertaking, the idea behind it was very simple, as an Aggressor explains:

Patch of the 65th Aggressor Squadron, based along with the companion 64th at Nellis.

The Red Baron report was formed with the sole purpose of analyzing everything that happened in all those air-to-air engagements—whether it resulted in a shoot-down didn't matter, just the fact that we had an air-to-air engagement—to find out how the guys were trained for that, and what the training actually did for them. And, based on that analysis, to come up with some recommendations.

Although the details of Red Baron are still secret, the major conclusions of the report have been discussed in open sources. Some of the findings were surprising, but most were basic laws of air combat, somehow forgotten and painfully relearned over Vietnam.

Take, for example, the fact that most attacks upon aircraft were unobserved by the target. In past wars, most aces have estimated about eight

Northrop F–5E Aggressor birds are prepared for a Red Flag "go" at Nellis.

out of ten of their victims never knew they were being attacked until it was too late. This figure was consistent in Vietnam; a former Aggressor pilot, who has presumably read the Red Baron findings, writes "approximately 80 percent of our losses were from unseen MiGs."

Although some analysts had thought that radar would make sneak attacks obsolete, it had the opposite effect. The North Vietnamese pilots, operating over their own territory under positive GCI control, were vectored into advantageous positions from which to jump the Americans. And most American pilots, used to training against

Aggressor jock casually awaits last-minute adjustment to his F–5E; bird is dressed in blue Warpac camouflage.

other USAF pilots in similar, larger aircraft — usually F–105s or F–4s, both immense for fighters — found it hard to pick up the smaller, more agile MiG–21s and MiG–17s, and sync themselves into the rhythm of the quicker dogfighters. Also, American pilots were not only effectively ignorant of the performance characteristics of the Frescoes and Fishbeds, they were also unfamiliar with the tactics employed by the enemy, who did not fight like Americans.

Some solutions to these problems were addressed in the Red Baron interim report, and are paraphrased here by the 64th Aggressor's CO:

First, we needed to change our air-to-air training profiles to make them more realistic. We had to start training our pilots in some large number scenarios where there were more bad guys than good guys, and in some tactical situations that would simulate what we knew to be happening, whether in North Vietnam or other parts of the world. We'd been doing a good job of that for training our guys to drop bombs, but we hadn't really been training the air-to-air pilot for the role he was involved in.

And we needed to come up with an airplane that we could train against, something similar to the Soviet aircraft and not similar to the U.S. aircraft.

Of course, the final thing we needed to do was to get a lot smarter than we were about the threat itself; talk to the Intel community, get the infor-

25

mation we needed to know—or at least ask the right kinds of questions—and get that information out to the field, get our fighter pilots smarter so that they could defeat the tactics and weaponry they were about to face.

Soviet MiG–21MF, an obsolete but still creditable all-purpose fighter which the Aggressor F–5 simulates.

The solution to these problems now seems obvious, but when the original Aggressor concept —a six-aircraft, six-pilot flight attached to the USAF Fighter Weapons School at Nellis—was briefed to the USAF chief of staff in 1972, it was a radical proposal (although, to be fair, the U.S. Navy had already come to the same conclusions in Top Gun). The concept quickly expanded from a flight to a full squadron, and on October 10, 1972, the 64th Fighter Weapons Squadron (later the 64th Aggressor Squadron) was formed at Nellis.

" 'To actively emulate the enemy in current fighter performance, tactics, and fighting philosophy'—that's our basic job," says the 64th's CO. "If we go out and do that the best way we know, then our guys can go out and develop counter-tactics to defeat the enemy if they go into combat for real."

On paper, it looks easy. After all, the Soviet fighter pilot does not set a high standard to live up to. He is taught to fly, not fight. On the other hand, the Aggressors are all highly trained, highly motivated volunteers with at least 500 hours of current fighter time (the equivalent of a full three-year tour in any USAF operational fighter). The Aggressor average is actually around 700 or 800 hours and approaches 2,000 hours when the records of the commander, ops officer, and the rest of the grizzled squadron vets are figured in. The competition is fierce; for your average, ambitious, young fighter jock, getting into the Aggressors is as tough as getting into Harvard.

"It's pretty tough to get in, simply because the numbers are so small," says an Aggressor pilot. "And there are a lot of air-to-air units in the TAF these days, especially with the F–15s. And we're not increasing our numbers that much, so there's a lot of people wanting to get in."

So when you reward these bright, young men for their initiative and dedication by sentencing them to impersonate pilots trained in a system where initiative is bred out, not in, they've got some major attitudinal adjustments to make. And sometimes it's hard.

"One of the basic mottoes of the Aggressors is 'Be Humble'," says a young 64th Aggressor jock.

And learning how to be humble takes a period of time. You've got guys coming in here that we've trained to be innovative and take the initiative, and we say, "Okay, so much for innovation, so much for initiative, now you're going to go out and fly these [Soviet] tactics that are probably going to result in your old buddy from your old squadron shooting you down. And you're just going to have to do your aileron roll to indicate you just got shot and died, and leave the fight. It's tough, but you've just got to bite the bullet."

A 65th Aggressor agrees life as an American MiG pilot takes some getting used to:

We fly no-fooling Soviet tactics, and we don't cheat on it. So we'll go out there and fly these Soviet tactics and some of them get us killed. You say, "Boy, I wouldn't do that if I was smart." But we're not allowed to be smart. So you've just got to be a Commie.

Although they are forced to live on a mixed diet of MiG Chow and humble pie, there's no shortage of applicants for the dozen slots in each of the three Adversary Tactics Instructor Courses taught at Nellis each year. Six pilots are trained at the 64th Aggressor Squadron, and the other six across the way at the 65th. When they complete their 41 training sorties and 121 formal academic hours of instruction, about half the graduates will remain at Nellis, with the 64th and 65th Aggressor Squadron, and the rest will be split between the two overseas Aggressor squadrons: PACAF's 26th Tactical Fighter Training Aggressor Squad-

ron, based at Clark AB in the Philippines, and the 527th TFTAS, USAFE's Aggressors, based at RAF Alconbury, in England.

When the Aggressor program began, most of the pilots came from Phantoms, primarily because what little practical air-to-air combat skill there was in the U.S. Air Force at that time resided in the F-4 squadrons. Since the introduction of the Eagle in the USAF inventory, a large number of new Aggressors are coming from F-15 squadrons, partly because those squadron assignments are booked solid and the Air Force is releasing those pilots to other assignments, and partly because the Eagle is a dedicated air-superiority fighter. So F-15 pilots are well acquainted with the air-to-air mission. But there are also Aggressor pilots from just about every other type of USAF squadron, including A-10, F-111, A-7. And now they're even getting some pilots with F-16 experience.

A lot of the Nellis Aggressors used to go on to the PACAF or USAFE Aggressor squadrons when their three-year tour was up, but that's being discouraged now. The Air Force wants to get the Aggressors back into the operational units, where their experience is helpful in training new pilots. They also want to give other pilots a chance to fly with the Aggressors. There has been talk of establishing an East Coast Aggressor Squadron—most likely at Tyndall AFB, in Florida—to cut down on deployment time, relieve some of the pressure on the Nellis Aggressors, and take advantage of the good weather and the ACMI (Air Combat Maneuvering Instrumentation) range over the Gulf of Mexico. But that's "Rumor Control."

"That idea comes and goes," says an Aggressor jock who flew in PACAF.

They're also discussing moving the squadron in PACAF to a different base, to cut down on deployment time and increase the number of sorties. The initial move, I'm sure, costs a bunch of money. But how long is it going to take you to recoup the money you lost moving them? If it takes six years,

maybe by that time you don't simulate the threat anymore.

But any expansion in the Aggressor program would be welcomed, both by the pilots themselves and the units they fly against.

"I think there's more demand for Aggressors now than there used to be," says a 65th Aggressor now on his second tour.

We used to just go out to units that had a higher priority. Now we'll go fly with the Air National Guard and the Air Force Reserve—everybody wants to get the training. Now you've got more people making demands on the same number of resources you started out with.

The Aggressors spend a great deal of time on the road. Over half of the 13,000-odd sorties the two Nellis Aggressor squadrons fly each year are

Scale silhouettes show relative sizes of MiG-21 *(upper left),* F-5 *(upper right),* F-4 *(lower left),* F-15 *(lower right).*

off the base, and at any given time almost a third of their aircraft and pilots are deployed, providing realistic training to other tactical air units at their bases. A typical Aggressor "road show" consists of six aircraft, eight pilots, a GCI controller, and seventeen maintenance personnel. The Aggressor pilots fly their planes to the deployment base, but for cost reasons the rest of the package will travel by road if the site is on the West Coast, or aboard a C-130 for longer trips.

The pilots will do more than fly at the road shows. Each Aggressor is assigned an area of academic expertise when he enters training and is obliged to put together a lecture on the subject, using up-to-date information processed through the 4513th Threat Training Group, the clearinghouse for intelligence information at Nellis. The briefings, all classified, deal with the following subjects:

The Soviet Fighter Pilot—The background and training of the Soviet fighter pilots and their allies. The lecture touches on his schooling, flight training, how he rises through the Soviet military hierarchy and, reportedly, gets pretty personal.

Frontal Aviation—The organization and capabilities of the Soviet battlefield air arm; FA is the Russian "equivalent" to the USAF's Tactical Air Command.

Formations and Tactics—Perhaps the most popular briefing, this deals with what the Flogger and Fishbed drivers are up to these days.

Specific Theater Threats—On request, the Aggressors will put together a briefing dealing specifically with one particular area of operations. If a squadron is about to be posted to South Korea, for example, the Aggressors can write a briefing on the potential air threats in the region.

The Future Threat—Probably the most sensitive briefing, this is a look at what the Soviet Union is coming up with in terms of new aircraft and equipment, according to various intelligence sources. This is reportedly a real "nuts and bolts" lecture dealing with the specific type of information American fighter pilots need to know.

Command and Control—Another sensitive subject, concerned primarily with the radar and GCI network supporting Soviet air operations in general, and the MiG-21 in particular.

This last briefing, usually given by the Aggressor's own GCI controllers, points out their importance to the Aggressor program. Since the Soviets rely heavily on ground control, it stands to reason the Aggressors would also emphasize GCI, and their controllers are an integral part of the unit. In fact, the Aggressor squadron is patterned after a regular American squadron of four flights, with one exception: there is a fifth flight, consisting entirely of GCI controllers, who closely direct all Aggressor flights.

"We know that the Russians, especially in their operations with the MiG-21, are very dependent on the ground-based radar controlling their aircraft to the fight," says an Aggressor CO. "We are just as dependent as they are on these guys on the ground getting us to the fight."

The Aggressor GCI controllers are also trained at Nellis. The Adversary Tactics Controller Course consists of seventy-seven academic hours and directing twenty-two air-to-air missions. Aggressor controllers also fly often, usually in the backseat of a F-5F. For a while there were no F-5Fs or T-38s in the Aggressor inventory, but recently the Aggressors took delivery of six brand new two-seat F-5F trainers. The flights give the controllers a perspective on what's really going on in the air and the type of information the pilot needs to know in a dogfight. It also helps dispel in the pilots the prejudice jocks traditionally have toward "scope-dopes." The Aggressor GCI controllers are the elite of their field—they wear the same uniforms as the pilots, are present at every briefing and debriefing, and are considered an equal, vital part of the team.

It's not the Aggressor's job to teach the pilots they fly against how to beat them step-by-step. Their job is to talk about the enemy on the ground and fly like him in the air. Advice on how to counter various enemy tactics is usually left to the Fighter Weapons School graduate, the squadron's weapons and tactics officer—he's the expert on the aircraft the Aggressor's opponents are flying.

But on the whole, the pilots teach themselves, through experience, what works against the Aggressors and what doesn't. After all, that's the point behind the program anyway—to give the line jocks experience in a near-combat situation. They might get "killed" in the first couple of missions;

that's okay. They usually wind up winning in the end.

"The learning curve starts way down there and then it goes—WHRRRR!" The 64th Aggressor pilot draws a parabola in the air.

We'll go out there the first couple of days, and we'll taxi on into people's six o'clock, and they won't see us. We'll take pictures of them on our gun camera film, shoot 'em, kill 'em, do all those kinds of things. And then we'll all debrief that after the fact.

It doesn't take too awful long—a couple of days—that guy gets a little embarrassed among all the other guys because all he had to do was look over his shoulder and he probably would have seen us. So he starts looking over his shoulder, paying a lot more attention to the overall threat: Ta-da! *He sees us! And defeats our attack, and then all of a* sudden *we end up on the defensive. Usually we come out much better at the beginning of the week than we do at the end of the week. In many air-to-air units who have had constant exposure to the Aggressors, right off the bat we're getting our knickers ripped. And that's good. That's what we like to see, that's why we're in business.*

The thing progresses from us doing real good, to them seeing us and defeating whatever attack we've got, to the last two or three days where they're taking the fight to us. Now we're not even getting to swing what we call their "three-nine line" (the target's rear hemisphere). *They're attacking us in the front quarter where we're getting killed, which is what we're supposed to do.*

"Normally, the first thing that a unit has to overcome is a proficiency problem," says another 64th AS pilot.

If they haven't fought the Aggressors for a while, the first thing they have to do is be able to find the threat. And it's different looking for different-size airplanes. You actually train your eyeballs to see different sizes; you make up your mind what you're looking for, then you look for that threat.

The next thing is a type of proficiency flying against Soviet tactics—we're structured a little more concretely in what we do than if they were fighting their own people. So the first few days it's usually a proficiency problem, and/or a communications problem, and as they start to learn that, they get better and better. Then it gets very hard for us to come out alive in a lot of those fights.

The Aggressors are very big on briefings and debriefings. And the way an applicant handles himself among other pilots has a lot to do with whether or not he'll get to wear the red star on his right shoulder.

"We feel that about 50 percent of all the value of any training sortie is gained on the debrief," says one Aggressor. "When you put it all together, whether on the blackboard or with your hands, you identify what went right and what went wrong, and what you can do to fix it next time."

Sometimes that's a lot harder than it sounds. Reconstructing an air-combat engagement bears a distressing resemblance to reconstructing the cause of an aircraft accident. Each participant has his own Rashomon-like tale of what went on, but the truth—what happened, why it happened, who thought he won, who really won and why—is difficult to pick up among the clutter of egos, solipsism and honest misperceptions. Before the Aggressors, in the Dark Ages of air-to-air training when the only dogfighting allowed was unauthorized hassling, the "victor" was usually the guy with the highest rank, loudest voice or greatest tolerance for liquor. Now, even specialists like the Aggressors often find they, too, have a less-than-perfect picture of what the fight was about.

"It's common to sit down with the other guys in your flight and come up with what you think happened," says an Aggressor from the 65th.

Fighter jocks rehash the afternoon's tussle before unsuiting in the Red Flag equipment room.

Then we get together with the guys we were flying against and usually find out neither side was exactly correct on what really happened. You have to put the two together.

I've had missions where I thought, "Boy, we really did good," and then found out later we were all "dead" before we ever did it.

"Everyone has their own slanted view of what happened," says an F-15 pilot who has flown against the Aggressors.

We all have to hash it out on the blackboard. It takes us a good deal of time and chalk-drawing to figure out exactly what happened. It takes so long *to do that!*

Aggressors strive to keep their face-to-face debriefs with the pilots they just flew against from getting personal, even to the point of referring to themselves by their call signs or "The F-5."

The planes the Aggressors fly are as well known as the pilots themselves. The Northrop F-5E Tiger II is flown operationally around the world, but

Navy and Marine fighters, such as this landing F/A-18, often join the Aggressors on the enemy side of the Red Flag air war.

the Air Force uses it exclusively as a tackling dummy. The F-5E—also known as the "MiG-5" or the "F-5 Humiliator" among USAF fighter jocks —is an extremely interesting aircraft, both for its capabilities and for its limitations, and deserves close inspection.

The F-5's ancestry goes all the way back to the Korean War, to the N-102 Fang, a rival of the Lockheed F-104 Starfighter. Powered by a single General Electric J-79 engine (which later went on to fame in the F-4), the Fang, with its high-mounted delta wing and swept horizontal stabilizers, bore a suspicious resemblance to the MiG-21. The N-102 was never produced, but its influence was evident in Northrop's subsequent N-156 Tally-Ho project, a lightweight fighter powered by a pair of GE J-85 engines (which were originally developed

for the USAF's Quail ECM decoy missile carried by SAC B–52s). The N–156 had its origins in a Navy requirement for a fighter that could operate from its smaller "jeep" carriers. Even though the Navy later canceled the program, the discipline involved in designing an aircraft for carrier use certainly contributed to the F–5's neat design.

Although the Navy had no use for the N–156, the Air Training Command was in the market for a new trainer. In 1958 the first flight of the T–38, the two-seat version of the N–156, signaled the beginning of the Talon's long and distinguished career in the USAF. More than a thousand T–38s were built between 1961 and 1972, and were used not only by the USAF, USN, and NASA, but also by the air forces of West Germany, Portugal, and Turkey.

The single-seat version, the N–156F, was later developed into the F–5A Freedom Fighter and offered to friendly nations under the U.S. Government's Military Assistance Program. Although the F–5 has never quite caught on operationally with

Aggressor F–5s sport almost a dozen different paint and camouflage schemes. Large Soviet-style nose numbers repeat last digits of tail code.

the USAF, it has been sold or produced in more than thirty countries. Only the MiG–21, an aircraft that the F–5 closely resembles, both physically and philosophically, serves in more air forces—thirty-six in all. The North Vietnamese air force still flies both types.

F–5As were operated by the air force of South Vietnam, and during the war the USAF experimented with a dozen modified Freedom Fighters in the ground attack role. The aircraft in the program, dubbed "Skoshi Tiger" ("skoshi" is a bastardization of *sokoshi*, the Japanese word for "small"), were fitted out with Navy-style refueling probes, armor plate, jettisonable bombing racks, and camouflage finishes. Ultimately, the USAF decided to pass on the aircraft, but the name "Tiger" was kept for the subsequent development of the F-5, the F-5E, which won the U.S. International Fighter Aircraft contest against three "paper" aircraft designs.

Compared with the F-5A, the Tiger II has more powerful engines, larger leading edge extensions, maneuver flaps, more fuel capacity, and an improved radar and gunsight. It is also slightly larger and heavier, although still not in the same size and weight class with current U.S. fighters. (The F-16 is an exception, and "Ghost" camouflaged F-5s are often mistaken for F-16s at Red Flag.)

When the Red Baron report recommended the use of a dissimilar aircraft in training American pilots, the Aggressors had the F-5E in mind all along. At first they had to settle for T-38s, though. The Talons, on long-term loan from the Air Training Command, displayed good service. But in terms of overall performance, and especially acceleration and weapons capability, the trainers were inferior to the F-5E, as well as to the aircraft they were emulating, the MiG-21. Ironically, the DACT (Dissimilar Air Combat Training) program got a boost when the *real* Aggressors, the North Vietnamese, overran the country and the F-5Es earmarked for the VNAF wound up at Nellis.

Aggressor pilots are quite happy with their little "scooter," which they find simple to operate and fun to fly. They are especially fond of the automatic maneuver flaps and the leading edge extensions, which can be combined to make the aircraft do some tricky stunts. When the pilot pushes a switch on the throttle quadrant back to "maneuver," the flaps are automatically trimmed to the best position to execute whatever maneuver the pilot is calling for. The leading edge extensions lower the aircraft's stall speed and contribute to the F-5E's ability to pull its nose up and point it at another aircraft in a slow speed dogfight.

A typical Aggressor trick: when he finds himself running out of airspeed while chasing, for example, an F-15 across the sky in a turning dogfight (quite routine), and the Eagle pilot decides to separate

in the vertical where he would normally be safe from his panting opponent, the leading edge slats and the automatic maneuvering flaps allow the Aggressor pilot to pull the F-5's nose up and point it at the F-15. Even though the Aggressor pilot can't begin to climb or do anything about the Eagle, this scares young lieutenants to death, and they pull their noses back down into the F-5 to negate that bluff, back to where the Tiger can still bite. This is called the "Standard Aggressor Brown Bar Conversion," although its exact Soviet designation is unknown.

The F-5 is quite maneuverable, especially in the horizontal plane. Its corner velocity, the speed at which the aircraft makes its quickest, tightest turn, is about 370 knots at 15,000 feet. By way of comparison, the F-4 corners at about 100 knots faster. Instantaneous turn rate—the maximum turning rate regardless of energy loss, good for putting the nose on the target or jinking the tail away from an attacker—is almost eighteen degrees a second, and the F-5E can sustain a turn rate of about ten degrees a second. G restrictions on the F-5E are exactly the same as for the F-15: from -3 G to +7.3 G. Only the phenomenal F-16 has better G performance: from -2 G to +9 G.

The F-5E is also quite fast, even at low altitude. Aggressors have been known to chase aircraft close to the deck at over 700 knots, but not often; the pilot burns up a lot of gas zooming around like that, and normal speeds are usually much lower. The Aggressors are fuel-limited enough as it is. The F-5E is not air-refuelable, and the aircraft can't fight with its centerline tank, so F-5 drivers can't afford to go jetting around the desert at the speed of sound for very long.

The visibility out of the cockpit is good, compared with other fighters of its generation, but the view is not as panoramic as in the modern "Teen-series" fighters. Aggressors are always rolling their aircraft in a "belly-check," looking for bandits under the F-5's long, flat nose. Rearward visibility

is even more restricted—about the same as an F-4 backseater's—which accounts for the Aggressors' nervous habit of kicking the aircraft's tail around to check six.

The F-5E's radar leaves a lot to be desired. Although the ranges are respectable for a light fighter—twenty miles maximum search, ten miles maximum lock-on—the radar has no off-boresight lock-on capability. This means the pilot must know where the bandit is, either visually or from a fairly precise plotting from a GCI controller, because the target must be pinned squarely in the pipper to be locked on. And because the F-5E's radar has no angle-track capability, the pilot must *keep* the target in the pipper to maintain his radar lock-on. The F5E's radar severely limits the Aggressors' ability to simulate beyond-visual-range radar missile combat.

On the other hand, Aggressor pilots love their gunsight, which they find very accurate and stable.

Aggressor F-5s in four different paint schemes head for a 4 vs. 4 fight over the range.

And quick—the Aggressors love to take snapshots, and almost every type of aircraft in the Free World has starred in their 16mm gun camera film. (The Aggressors would be in bad shape if they had to shoot real bullets instead of film. The ammunition box for their port 20mm cannon is routinely removed to provide space in the gun bay for the pilot's luggage on road trips!) The Aggressors would prefer to use videotape instead of film for two reasons. For one thing, videotape is instantaneous, but film must be processed, and that usually takes at least half a day. Most modern USAF squadrons use videotape and are not set up to process film. So the Aggressors don't use their gun camera film in the face-to-face briefing but rely instead on the Walkman-like audiotape recorders they stash inside their map cases during flight.

F-5Es are not certified to carry the wing-tip tanks carried by the F-5A and T-38. Instead, they usually carry a captive Sidewinder training missile —typically an AIM-9E or an AIM-9J, depending on the missile they're going to simulate—on one of the wing tips. It doesn't matter which wing tip, since there's no effect on the aerodynamic stability of the aircraft, even if the other wing tip is unloaded (although Aggressor F-5s often tote an AMCI pod on the other tip if they're flying on an Air Combat Maneuvering Instrumentation range).

Much has been written about the F-5E's similarity to the MiG-21 Fishbed. The two aircraft are practically identical in the important aspects: wing loading, acceleration, and turning ability. Most importantly, they are almost the same size (small), and both have smokeless engines. On the other hand, the MiG's engine is stronger in terms of pure thrust, and the Fishbed maneuvers better at

Air Combat Maneuvering Instrumentation (ACMI) pod for transmission of flight data to real-time ground display.

slower speeds. The biggest difference is in avionics. Later models of the MiG-21 have a more powerful radar, although Fishbed drivers would no doubt prefer the F-5's excellent gunsight to the one installed over their dashboards. In general, however, the differences are not significant, and the F-5E is an accurate MiG-21 simulator: "If a guy can beat an F-5," says one Aggressor, "he should be able to beat a MiG-21."

But the F-5 is a less accurate Flogger simulator. True, they are about the same size; with its wings cranked back, the variable-geometry MiG-23 actually has a *smaller* wingspan than the F-5, although the Flogger's boxy, ungraceful planform supposedly makes it easier to spot than an F-5. But there the performance of the two aircraft

diverges. The Flogger is a much faster aircraft, one of the fastest in the world. But it can't turn very well at all. In fact, the *F–4* would probably be a better Flogger simulator than the F–5, but even the Phantom has a better turning capability (plus it's too big and smokes too much). The MiG–23 is actually very close to the F–104 in performance, which is to say, it goes like a bullet and turns like one, too.

The Flogger is a very un-MiG-like MiG. The qualities normally associated with aircraft from the Mikoyan-Gurevich collective—low wing-loading, good horizontal maneuverability and less sophisticated avionics—are reversed in the Flogger. It is the first Soviet tactical fighter with a radar that must be taken seriously, although the High Lark radar in the MiG–23's nose cannot be compared with the radars in the F–15, or even the F–16, and is closer in capability to the type of radar carried

Inert AIM–9 Sidewinder lacks motor and warhead, but contains electronics for realistic simulated firing.

by the F–4E. (The latest MiG–23 variant, the Flogger–G, has a slightly more advanced radar, reportedly with some look-down, shoot-down capability, but still not up to modern Western standards.)

"The Soviets are always filling gaps," says an Aggressor whose academic specialty is the MiG–23. "They needed an airplane that could work autonomously, that could have its own capability to get to the fight if GCI crumps, or they get jammed, or whatever. It's a step from going with herds of simple, dumb airplanes."

Since the MiG–23 is not much like the MiG–21, it stands to reason that the F–5E, which is such a good Fishbed simulator, would have a tough time giving a creditable Flogger impression. The Aggressors can, and do, fly Flogger tactics in their

F-5s, but the BVR (Beyond Visual Range) capability of the Flogger and its AA-7 Apex missile is tough for them to simulate. The F-5's radar was not meant for BVR fighting, and the Aggressors sometimes have to work in concert with their GCI controllers to accurately portray Flogger/Apex attacks. (Just for the record, the maximum/minimum ranges of the simulated Apex radar envelope given to Red Flag players in the Mass Brief are: Face-to-face—7 mi/2 mi, On the beam—4 mi/ 1 mi, Rear hemisphere (stern) —2 mi/ ½ mi.)

Sometimes, when other aircraft are brought in to play on the OPFOR side during Red Flag (usually Navy or Marine F-4s), they are designated "Flogger" simulators, but this is a misnomer. Although the added numbers and the BVR radar missile threat contribute to the realism of the scenario, the aircraft do not try to emulate Flogger performance

F-15 Eagle dwarfs tiny F-5s. Its tail span is actually larger than the wing span of the Tiger II.

or Soviet tactics. They are not trained for it, and to try to do so would only serve to provide negative training to both sides. Although they may be deployed initially in a manner similar to how the Red forces feel Floggers might be used, they fly and fight like Americans.

The Aggressors don't try to emulate Foxbats, or Flagons, or any other type of Soviet aircraft, either. An Aggressor explains why:

Because we're limited in numbers, we try to define the scope. Right now, projected up to the near future, their [the average USAF fighter pilot] *chances of meeting a MiG-21 or a MiG-23 are extremely high, much higher than meeting a Fencer or a Fitter or something like that.*

Besides, it's probably more important to simulate threats than targets.

Yeah, it is. You try to simulate the worst case, and the most capable in terms of performance or avionics are the MiG–21 and the MiG–23, certainly in numbers. They can usually take care of the other stuff.

But what about the future? By now everyone has heard about the various new Soviet fighter designs, supposedly poised on the edge of production. Given the USAF's recent emphasis on getting intelligence information down to the fighter pilots who need to know it most, the Aggressors, and especially those pilots who brief the newest Soviet threat as their academic specialty, should certainly have a good idea of what's coming up. Although they can't talk much about it, one thing is clear: the next generation of Soviet fighters will continue the trend started with the Flogger—

Aggressor F–5 closes unseen on the six-o'clock of a Blue Force F–15.

larger airframes, and more advanced avionics and weapons system capability. If the F–5 is hard-pressed today to provide a realistic Flogger threat, it is bound to have a tough time emulating the more advanced Soviet jets, if and when they enter service. But the Aggressors have no concrete plan for an aircraft to replace or even supplement the F–5E.

"I suspect we're going to be flying the F–5E for a long time," an Aggressor says.

It's a money thing. It would cost a lot of bucks to design and build a new airplane that would be totally an Aggressor airplane. I think probably what you'll see in the future is us continuing to fly the F–5E, maybe making some modifications to it to

*make it a better avionics threat. Performance-
wise, it's still a good airplane.*

*Ten years from now, we're probably going to
see a shift towards a different kind of airframe with
some significantly different performance and avionics capabilities that's probably very similar to
what our F-15s and F-16s have today. It could
very well be that ten years down the road, one of
our normal airplanes that we have out there in
operational units now might very well be a reasonable simulator. But that's all dependent upon what
they really develop and really put into operation.
We can hypothesize a lot of things, but we'll have
to wait and see what they went with.*

There was at one time a widespread assumption
that the Aggressors would receive the newest
version of the F-5, the F-20 Tigershark (instantly
dubbed "Gomershark," by Aggressor jocks;
"gomer" meaning bad guys in a general sense,
and Soviets, specifically). But cost is a major factor. It's hard to rationalize the introduction of a
brand new fighter into the USAF inventory, especially if it's never going to fight. For the same reason, there are no plans for the Aggressors to
adopt the "Dial-a-Threat" version of the F-16/79,
a lower-powered Fighting Falcon with a built-in
computer that limits its pilots to the performance
characteristics of the aircraft being simulated.
(One Aggressor pilot whimsically says the Air
Force should buy a couple of F-20s, paint them
like regular Aggressor F-5Es, and, when the Eagle
sneaks up behind the Gomershark, thinking he's
dealing with a regular Tiger, the Aggressor can
"light up the burner and surround him with one airplane.")

But the Aggressors don't necessarily need
higher performance, just performance more accurately reflecting the threat they're simulating. In
this respect, there are a couple of aircraft that are
much better Flogger simulators. The Mirage F-1 is
a good Flogger simulator, as is the Israeli Kfir. In
fact, the Kfir was, for a time, thought of as a dark

horse candidate for an F-5E supplement. That
was before America's recently strained relations
with the Israelis. But a new Aggressor aircraft
would be a good place for the United States to
prove it means what it says about weapons pro-
curement being a two-way street with our allies.

The F-5Es of each squadron are painted in
camouflage schemes similar to those used by
Soviet units or their allies. Similar is the key word
here; those nasty Russkies refuse to send paint
chips, and the pilot at each Aggressor squadron
who is detailed to reference threat paint-schemes
often winds up "eyeballing" the paint mix from a
photograph. As any scale modeler will tell you, this
is tricky business.

"It's not imagination so much as it's trying to get
the paint to come out exactly the way it's supposed to come out," says one frustrated Aggressor artist.

*You sit there and say, "Well, we put brown with
this much red, and it should come out this color."
And you mix it up, and you say, "Well, it doesn't
look bad in the can, you know; let's paint a piece
of metal." And you hold it up, and it doesn't look
bad, so you say, "Let's go with those proportions."*

*Well, sure as hell, you throw it on an airplane,
and what was supposed to be dark brown comes
out purple. The intent is to make them as abso-
lutely accurate as we can, and some of them are.
The others that aren't—it's just a problem with the
paint mix and the sun and all this other stuff.*

One of the paint schemes that got away is the
infamous Nellis "Banana"; not even the Soviets
would court aerial embarrassment by camou-
flaging their aircraft in signal green and day-glo
yellow.

*That was a mistake. That was supposed to be
what we call a "pumpkin," which was going to
come out an orangish and brown type of thing. We
screwed up—it came out looking like a banana.*

Aggressor pilots call it the "designated mort"
and groan whenever they're detailed to fly it,

Aggressor pilot scans instruments after engine start.

which isn't that often; for some reason the Banana has a history of small problems that often render it unflyable, a suspicious trait in the usually reliable F–5E. Perhaps the reason can be discerned by this excerpt, given to Red Flag players by the Red Flag commander discussing the Aggressor F–5s:

They've also got one out there that looks like a bruised banana—you can see that miles and miles away. Seven miles away you get a Tally-ho on that airplane, and you'd swear it wasn't an F–5, but go ahead and kill that guy anyway.

The Aggressors try to keep a representative balance of the different kinds of paint schemes found on MiGs all over the world. "Pull out the good old *Jane's All the World's Aircraft*," laughs an Aggressor. "You'll see all the different colors, all the ones we've got, and where they came from."

Ironically, Nellis Aggressors are "lucky" that the Middle East is such a volatile area, because the camouflage finishes that work over the Golan, say, or over the Bekaa Valley are also very effective at low altitude in the Great Basin. But others aren't so effective in the desert; the new "Blue" scheme may be perfect over the Baltic Sea for the Soviet Fishbed jocks (from whom the Aggressors "borrowed" the color), but it's not the kind of thing you'd want to wear if you're skulking down low through Cedar Pass, trying to sneak up on some Eagle driver. Likewise, the "Gray" scheme is just the ticket for the Leningrad Military District, for which it was developed. It's one of the Aggres-

sor's favorite finishes for high-altitude work; however, it's easy to spot down low against the brown and tan of the Nevada wasteland.

Sometimes it works the other way. There aren't many deserts in the United States, and when the Aggressors go on the road they often find themselves painfully conspicuous in "Lizard," "Sand," or "Snake" camouflage.

"We like to employ our camouflage tactically, also," says an Aggressor jock. "So, for example, if we're flying over water I *do not* like to fly in a sand-colored F-5."

Still, the Aggressors are very busy these days, and there's barely enough F-5s to go around. They don't have the luxury of picking the airplane

to match the mission and have to make do with what they've got. If they're going to try to sandwich someone high and low, for example, they might send the "dirty" F-5s down on the deck and keep the grays and blues at altitude.

The Aggressors have nicknames for each of the camouflage finishes. The nicknames may vary from squadron to squadron—as may the exact finishes, after each squadron plays its own game of Paint Chip Roulette—but the camouflage schemes are fairly consistent throughout the USAF Aggressor community. These are from the 64th Aggressor Squadron:

Pumpkin—Ugly, two-tone dark green and brownish yellow, similar to Warsaw Pact camou-

flage. "Banana" is an unwelcome "Pumpkin" variation.

Gomer—Similar to the three-tone USAF Vietnam-era camo still found on most F-4Es, but with steel gray in place of the dark green. This was actually VNAF standard finish for F-5s.

Lizard—Tan and chocolate desert camouflage; very effective at low altitude on the Nellis ranges.

Sand—Like "Lizard," but with light green added. "Sand" along with "Blue" are perhaps the prettiest Aggressor finishes.

Snake—Again, like "Lizard," except with dark green and a rustier brown. This is a favorite Flogger finish and is called "the Frog" by USAFE Aggressors.

Left: Jammed Red Flag ramp appears at top center of this aerial view of Nellis AFB. *Above:* F-5 with "snake" finish is readied for late-morning joust.

Ghost—Similar to modern USAF Compass Ghost Gray fighters, but with three shades of gray instead of two; very effective air-to-air finish, and the Aggressor's all-purpose choice.

Gray—Like the F-15's finish. Sometimes called "Total Gray" because the entire aircraft is painted gray—even the dielectric radome (which is unusual for Aggressor F-5s, but almost standard for the Navy's Top Gun F-5s, which have no radar).

Blue—A striking three-toned blue, good for fighting over water; similar to the Top Gun finish

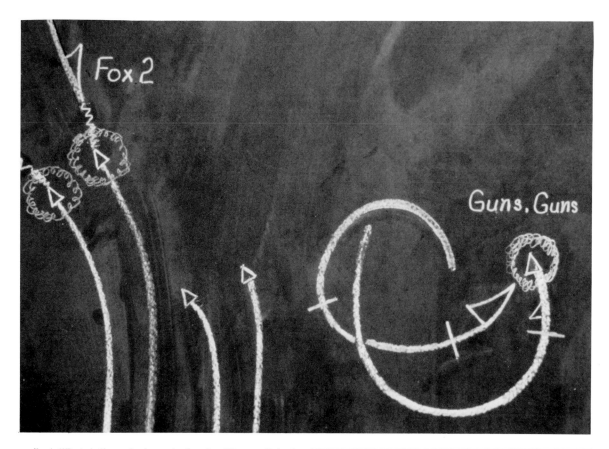

Elaborate multicolored chalk diagrams help Aggressors recreate the flight for debrief with Blue Force pilots.

called "Patch," and also similar to "Grape," but much less purple and intense.

Silver—Natural metal, with a flat black radome and anti-glare panel forward of the cockpit. Next to the Banana, this is the Aggressor's least-favorite finish.

Silver Gray—Almost identical to "Silver," but the aircraft is painted with silver dope instead of being left bare metal.

Although the garish camouflage on the Aggressors' F–5s first catches the eye, the markings on the aircraft are also quite nonstandard. To begin with, they are the only fighters in the USAF inventory to sport huge "buzz numbers" on both sides of the nose. These are, of course, part of their

Soviet disguise, and are standard issue on Floggers and Fishbeds around the world. The numbers on the nose correspond to the last two digits of the aircraft's serial number, which is repeated in full on the tail (where most USAF fighters carry only the last three digits).

The Aggressor buzz numbers come in a variety of colors. The most common scheme at Nellis is red trimmed with yellow; but there are also Aggressor F–5s with red numbers and black borders, blue with white trim, and yellow edged in black.

Some aircraft have three-digit buzz numbers, but this seems to be a function of the particular camouflage finish and not, as has been reported, merely to distinguish between two aircraft with the same two last digits in their serial numbers.

Nellis F–5s carry a full-color TAC insignia on the tail, but their markings are far from Tactical Air Command standard. Unlike most USAF fighters, they carry no tail code, neither the "WA" of the Fighter Weapons School, nor the "NA" of the 474th TFW, Nellis' resident F–16 wing. They do sport a tail-header, the famous yellow and black checkerboard pattern of the 57th Fighter Weapons Wing. They also carry the wing's patch on their intakes, just aft of the primary position lights.

F–5s of the 64th Aggressors marshall before commencing 4 vs. 4 fight with Holloman Eagles.

In an era of low-contrast, low-visibility markings, when most fighters have gone to the gray or black outline star-and-bar, the Aggressor's F–5s still carry the full-color national insignia. And even though most USAF planes don't even have "USAF" written on them anymore, the Aggressors, the most anti-American of all American fighter units, spell it out: "U.S. Air Force," top, bottom, and on both sides. Apparently, this is for safety reasons; after all, these things look like MiGs, fly like MiGs, and go around bothering American

45

Left: Aggressors rely on hand signals during startup, since Aggressor birds lack ground intercoms. *Above:* Gomer-in-training climbs in for practice hop.

fighters. How would you like to be an Aggressor pilot in USAFE with a broken radio, no ammo, and indistinguishable national markings, trying to tell a Dutch interceptor pilot—with hand signals yet—that even though the airplane you're flying looks a lot like those "see and avoid" planforms they have tacked up at his squadron headquarters, you are really an American, and he's about to make a big mistake? The Aggressors never go *near* real MiGs anyway, but the big markings are just insurance.

Each Aggressor pilot has his name stenciled on the canopy rail of an F–5E. However, as is the case with every fighter unit, since he takes the plane the maintenance people tell him to take, if he ever flies "his" plane, it's only coincidence. Some maintenance people have their names on the aircraft as well.

Sometimes markings just *show up* on the aircraft. Fighter pilots love two things: practical jokes and themselves. So it's a rare Aggressor aircraft that returns from a road trip without being attacked at least once by a less-than-sober fighter pilot armed with a stencil and a can of spray paint. At best, the F–5 will come away with the insignia of the squadron the pilot has just flown against plas-

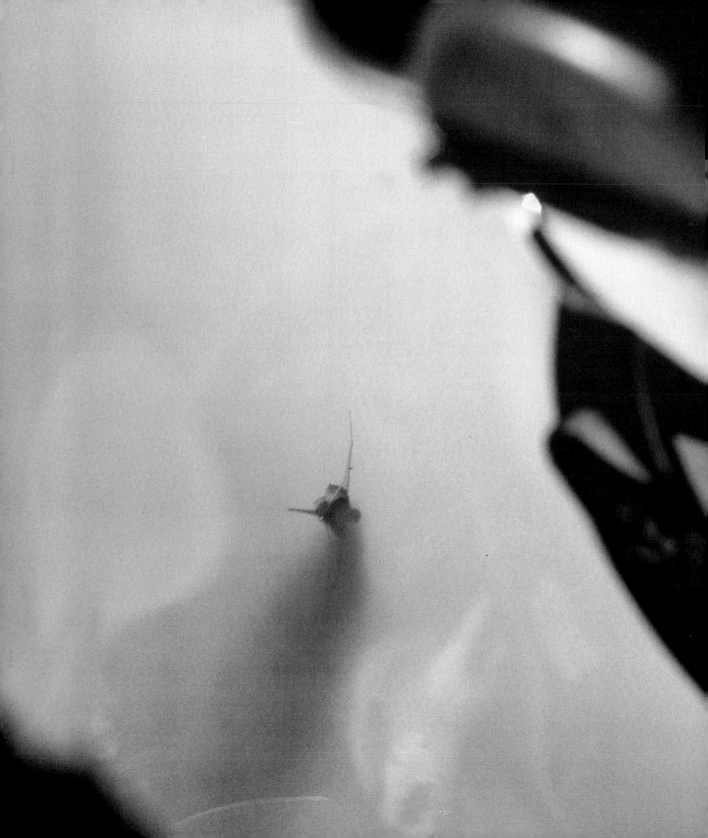

Left: "Better check your six, pal." Above: Aggressor two-ship climbs out from Nellis for the Red Flag range.

tered on the fuselage. But some of the graffiti is just plain manly derision: "Eagle Meat" is a favorite epithet sprayed on the F-5s by F-15 drivers. The Aggressor's only recourse is to retaliate by sneaking out one night (just like a bunch of Commies!) and painting "MiG Chow" on an Eagle's intake.

Since the real-life MiG drivers are starting to go to wraparound camouflage, the Aggressors are beginning to paint the undersides of their F-5s as well. But if you look close enough on the nose-gear door of any F-5 with white undersides, you will see a small, red star.

Not all Aggressor F-5Es are identical. Some are equipped with an Instrument Landing System (distinguishable by the flat ILS cap on the tip of the tail), and some that were used in the AIMVAL/ACEVAL tests have been modified to use the latest generation of Sidewinder missiles.

But no Aggressor F-5E has a pilot-to-ground crew intercom or an air-conditioning system that functions when the plane is on the ground. The Aggressors have turned these limitations into an asset, and the flight line *pas de deux* between F-5 pilot and crew chief is an impressive sight.

The crew chief must use hand signals to communicate with the pilot. He does this with great enthusiasm, sweeping the sky with wide cheerleader gestures. When the chocks are pulled, the Aggressor pilot shoots his arm out the open canopy and gives the crew a "thumbs up" pointing at the sky. The whole business looks like a Thunderbird launch; corny and somehow stirring, but not easily forgotten. It's ironic, in these days of cosmic avionics and automatic weapons systems, that the last fun, eyeball-to-eyeball, all-American, Big Sky, full-time yanking and banking flying is done by a unit pretending to be Commies.

"Sometimes it's tough being a Gomer," says an Aggressor pilot. "But I don't care—it's the best flying in the Air Force."

Chapter 3
FAM Hop

When the Players come to Red Flag, their first mission is always a familiarization ride —called a "FAM Hop"—a half-speed tour of the Nellis ranges to get a good look at the geography that had been, up to then, just scratches on a map. That sounds like a good idea; let's take a little FAM Hop ourselves.

Las Vegas is Spanish for "the meadows," a strange name for a place that, as one journalist notes, "could not support the merest form of vegetable life without a massive influx of Teamster funds." When there is wind, it's like dragon's breath. The soil is hard-packed and dry as chalk. Sharp, blue mountains ring the city, as if Las Vegas itself and everyone in it were caught in a giant bear trap, a leg on each jaw, and one step outside would shut that trap forever.

If Vegas seems inhospitable, it is paradise compared to the country around it. Nevada is the driest of all states. Out here they don't talk about how big a body of water is, just whether or not it's "permanent." The Great Basin, the vast desert and scrubland north of the city, is a curious juxtaposition of the relentless horizontal and the sudden vertical; there are ninety different mountain ranges in the Great Basin, and between them there is nothing at all.

There is life out there, most of it low and scaly: leopard lizards, horned toads, gopher snakes,

---

A-10 Warthog reloads 30mm gun on dry Texas Lake as part of Rapid Deployment Force scenario.

---

spiny lizards, desert iguanas, bull snakes, king snakes, Great Basin rattlers, sidewinders, and tarantulas. But there are some surprises. The Great Basin is home for the largest water bird wildlife refuge in the United States. There are mountain lions skulking up along the ridges. There are also some cattle, raised by ranchers on land leased from the U.S. Bureau of Land Management.

And there are even wild mustangs, 5,000 of them, living off the cheatgrass brome—"bronco grass"—a Mediterranean export that, unfortunately, causes many prairie fires out on the range. The mustangs have so far eluded all attempts to round them up. They like it out there around Grass Spring Canyon and have enough "horse sense" to stay out from under the falling bombs. "We've never seen a carcass," says a range officer.

The rest of the landscape is all scrubgrass and brush: mesquite, yucca, blackbrush, Joshua trees, creosote bush, and sagebrush. No doubt about it, it's Wily Coyote country, and a hell of a place to put America's Pleasure Dome. How did Las Vegas wind up here in the middle of nowhere?

By accident. Las Vegas was built by a salvo of booms. When Nevada was granted statehood in 1864, only the fifty or so Indians and miners who worked the valley were here to greet the travelers from the Rockies as they stopped at the oasis on their way to Southern California. But boom after boom of urban alchemists swept the valley—first silver, then gold, then the railroad, and the giant Boulder Dam project. Legalized gambling played a

big part, of course. And so did the sonic boom of the U.S. Air Force.

Red Flag ramp often holds 60-70 tactical birds.

The flyboys arrived in the form of the Army Air Corps, on January 25, 1941, when the mayor of Las Vegas signed over to the U.S. Army the land that would eventually become Nellis Air Force Base. It really wasn't all that much, just a dirt runway, a water well, and a dinky operations shack. But it's the thought that counts, and the Air Corps thought it would be a great place to put a gunnery school; the weather is excellent for flying and there was plenty of government land available for a dollar an acre. The land was cheap because it really wasn't much good for anything but gunnery practice—you could bomb it into oblivion and never notice the difference.

Las Vegas Army Air Field quickly grew—at one point it was turning out more than 800 B–17 crewmen every five weeks. The base shut down in 1947, but reopened again in 1949 as the Las Vegas Air Force Base, providing the new U.S. Air Force with advanced, single-engine training for its pilots. That mission changed when the United States got into the Korean War, and almost every American jet fighter pilot that stalked MiG Alley learned his stuff over the Great Basin.

When the Air Force changed the name of its bases to honor USAF heroes instead of geographic areas, Las Vegas Air Force Base became Nellis AFB in 1950. Lt. William Harrell Nellis was a sixty mission P–47 pilot from Clark County. He was killed on December 27, 1944, in Europe; he was twenty-eight years old.

Lieutenant Nellis would certainly be in awe of the base that bears his name today. It has more than 10,000 employees, with a payroll way over $100 million. It is the largest air base in the Tactical Air Command, and probably the busiest—it is a rare TAC pilot who has never seen Nellis AFB. By the main gate at Nellis, there is a small billboard. Although the illustration on the sign changes, the legend underneath always remains the same: "Welcome to Nellis Air Force Base—Home of the Fighter Pilot!"

If Nellis is home of the fighter pilot, then the fighter pilots' playroom has got to be Building 201. The 4440th TFTG headquarters, the Players' base of operations while at Red Flag, is a rather disappointing sight from the outside. The building seems too small and old, compared to what goes on inside it. They are building a much-needed

Main gate at Nellis AFB, Las Vegas.

addition in back, and when it is finished, many of the operations now conducted from mobile homes in the parking lot will be moved inside. The trailers are called temporary buildings, although they are little more than sparsely furnished, air-conditioning factories, and are mostly devoted to liaison operations from other commands.

The trailers are often indistinguishable from the outside. But there's no mistaking the headquarters of the Desert Survival School, with its lizards, snakes, and other little beasties caged outside the front door.

"I want you to know that all our Desert Aggressors are volunteers and are highly motivated individuals," a survival instructor says of his "pets."

53

"We have some of our better and more experienced instructors and evaluators caged up out there."

The survival instructors have been at Red Flag since the beginning. As part of the realistic scenario, pilots who were "shot down" at Red Flag used to be hauled out of their cockpits upon landing and helicoptered back to where they "ejected," to survive and help the rescue forces pick them up.

That's still the premise behind the Desert Survival School, but now the pilots who undergo the training are selected by their own units. This provides the school's ten instructors with a more consistent work load (What if nobody got shot down? What if *everybody* got shot down?) and spreads the training around. Otherwise, they might get the same students again and again, turning poor pilots

Marine AH-1 Cobra gunships take on mobile ground targets in concert with Air Force A-10s.

into great survivors—which, if you think about it, is probably not a bad idea. Besides, in the old involuntary days, "we had to go track them down," says an instructor, making them feel a little like bill collectors.

The instructors are all enlisted personnel from the Military Airlift Command's 3636th Combat Crew Training Wing at Fairchild AFB in Washington, where pilots also go for their seventeen-day "Advanced Boy Scout Camp," basic survival training. Like their lizards and snakes, the instructors are all highly motivated volunteers. "We have good retention and good esprit de corps," says an instructor, "because you have to go through so much garbage to become one."

The "victim"—usually a pilot or weapons system officer, but sometimes an enlisted tailgunner or loadmaster—is first given a briefing. He will set up authentication procedures to make sure the helicopter pilot he's talking with is the Real Thing and not an "enemy." (What's his dog's name? Who's his favorite baseball player?) Then he'll be given an intelligence briefing; the general area he was flying in when he got "shot down." Next he'll be given a safety briefing and some instructions on how to use the survival equipment. Then it's off to the desert either by helicopter or truck. There's always an instructor present, but the downed crewman is on his own.

"Throughout their whole career they've been listening to survival instructors talk to them," says an instructor. "But when they get here, they have to make their own decisions. They have to decide

Many Red Flags contain downed-pilot rescue missions, the job of Sikorsky "Jolly Green Giant" helicopters.

what they're going to do and when they're going to do it. And if they goof up, they're the ones that are going to pay for it."

Sometimes the pilots complain that the desert isn't a realistic place to practice survival skills; but an instructor says that's just agoraphobia, the fear of open spaces:

The desert is not a hard place to hide in. It's an extremely *difficult place to find somebody in.*

Finding the downed crewman is the job of the rescue forces, which are frequent visitors to Red Flag. The Air Force did a very good job of picking up pilots who ejected in Southeast Asia, and rescue crewmen rarely had to buy their own drinks at any officers' club in Vietnam. The rescue mis-

sion is so complex and expensive, it has been nicknamed "Picking up the President." It's not easy, either, and at Red Flag some instructors play the role of enemy soldiers trying to capture the pilot before the rescue forces can find him. They will try to confuse both the downed pilot and the rescue crewmen, and even use smoke, flares, and simulated hand grenades.

Pilots have a more serene afternoon at the school's Lake Mead operation, where they learn water survival. Sure, the instructors simulate parachute wind drag by dragging the poor pilot around behind a motorboat, but mainly they just stick him

Heavily loaded F-4 rolls inverted to begin descent for bomb run.

out in the middle of the lake for half a day: "When a man's sitting out there in a dinghy," says the school's CO, "he's got a lot of time to think."

Across the sweltering parking lot, Building 201 looks like any other Air Force office building— long, low, and nondescript. Even before you open the door, however, there is a preview of what's inside. The entrance to the building is plastered with stickers from and about anything that flies. Since Red Flag is the crossroads of the fighter pilot community, almost every unit comes to Nellis armed with mementoes of their presence, which they stick indiscriminately on any flat surface; the doorway of Building 201 and the walls of the men's room inside are favorite targets.

The theme is repeated, in a more formal fashion, along the square hallway inside. Every foot is covered with framed art, flying thank-you notes from the Players to the Red Flag staff, illustrated with photos, line art, and full-color paintings. Space is getting critical now that so many squadrons have gone through the Red Flag program. But nobody has the heart to take any plaques off the wall, so they are fast crowding out the "official" posters of enemy aircraft and antiaircraft threats. Hopefully the new building will be finished soon.

The duty desk is right inside the door on the left. There is nothing exceptional about it, except the following story:

Once upon a time, there was a made-for-TV movie called "Red Flag: The Most Dangerous Game," a highly unlikely tale in which Barry Bostwick, an F-4 pilot, brings his wife to Red Flag but leaves his Weapons Systems Operator at home. (There is a scene where his whizzo introduces himself to Bostwick on the flight line, much to the amusement of the Nellis boys.) Bostwick comes up with a "secret maneuver" to elude William Devane, an Aggressor pilot in every sense of the word, a man with the incisors of a puma and no discernible sense of humor. The plot soon lapses into pioneer mode, wandering off into several strange and new directions, but finally returns to a duel between Bostwick with his secret maneuver (which Phantom drivers everywhere instantly recognized as the Standard F-4 Double-handed Polish Heart Attack) and the terminally aggressive Mr. Devane. Being written for TV after all, the plot rapidly boils down to what the producers probably had in mind in the first place, a 600-mile-an-hour car chase using Buicks with wings (hence the F-4). The movie ends with Bostwick either leaving the Air Force or not (having left Devane, shall we say, deep into real estate north of Las Vegas). It doesn't matter anyway, because in the last scene Bostwick and his wife inexplicably march into the Nellis hospital for a much-needed rest. (He had been suffering from a case of the wimps.)

Anyway, the movie is still a sore spot at Nellis, especially among the brass who reportedly approved the script and then pulled a *violent* separation maneuver when they saw how Hollywood saw them. But a few enlisted guys manning the ops desk had the right attitude, and for weeks after the movie aired they answered the phone with a cheerful "Red Flag, the Most Dangerous Game," until they were told to cut it out.

The rest of the building is mostly devoted to cramped briefing rooms, although there are some other points of interest:

The Red Flag Intelligence Shop—The place looks rather like an insurance office, but on one wall there is a big map of the Nellis tactical ranges on which the "completely notional" but familiar-sounding 108th Guards Tank Army is spread across the FEBA (Forward Edge of the Battle Area), poised to take over Las Vegas.

The Auditorium—It's a big place, but it's filled during the mass briefings. The walls here, too, are lined with mementoes from units participating in past Red Flags. There is row after row of theater seats with fold-up-arm desks, but they still have to haul in Air Force blue folding chairs for the bigger briefings. The dais is flanked by two poorly designed slide screens (which doesn't matter, because the type on the slides is so small, you *have* to have fighter pilot eyes to read it). Surprisingly, there is no microphone. There is no clock either. But you always know what time it is at any Red Flag briefing because, every hour on the hour, the forty-dollar Casio Digital Alarm Chronograph-Calculators, uniformly worn by every fashion-conscious fighter jock, will engulf the auditorium in a wave of tiny beeps.

The 4440 TFTG Offices—The Red Flag CO's office is big, but cluttered. Like Building 201 itself, the office is partitioned into a rectangled walkway by a huge, oak table with drawers in it. The walls are covered with the inevitable airplane plaques, most of them from foreign outfits (either to give our allies a good impression, or maybe to stem complaints of favoritism from American units). The one that grabs visitors' attention is a framed poster depicting the RAF's Buccaneer, the world's ugliest aircraft, from every ugly angle. Buccaneer pilots are great favorites at the Nellis Officers' Club— American fighter jocks are respectful and amazed at their ability to push the ungainly Buc so fast and so low. How low? During one Red Flag, a Buccaneer pilot scratched out skid marks on the desert floor with his wing tip. On the same exercise, another Buccaneer lost its radome when it hit a power line, *climbing up!* The crews that went out to repair it came back with the news that the power line had been exactly forty-two feet off the ground. That's low. Both crews were fine, and No. 208 Buccaneer sported a power line "kill marking" shortly afterward.

The Snack Bar—Fighter pilots never seem to consume anything but beer and barbecued chicken wings (for which they will fly through thunderstorms); so even though the little Snack Bar doesn't offer much in the way of cuisine, it makes up for it in atmosphere. There are two huge murals, both in the style of Keith Ferris, the great aviation artist: an illustration of the USAF attack on the Paul Doumar Bridge in North Vietnam, and an F-111 takeoff. Covering the other walls is the handiwork of a fellow named Arkey Huber, who makes souvenir T-shirts for the squadrons who come to Red Flag. Huber is a famous Nellis character, an ex-B-17 crewman with a great affection for the Players, an affection that is mutual. The lounge is continuously jangled by the bleats and honks from not one but *two* "Astro-Fighter" machines, unanimously voted the video game "most

Cold-eyed Aggressor jocks evaluate ever-changing electronic threats in squadron rec room.

like a Fox 1 (radar missile) kill in an F-15." (Yes, fighter pilots love video games, too, and can't wait until somebody comes out with "Warsaw Pact-MAN.") In the corner there is a beer machine with carefully applied, press-type lettering reading "Jock Juice," "JP 3.2," and "Aircrew Debriefing Fluid." The pilots never patronize the beer machine during flying hours, although they all look as if they'd like to.

The Personal Equipment Room—This is where the Players stash their flying gear while at Red Flag. "PE" is across from the duty desk, next to the entrance. It doesn't look much different from the Personal Equipment room at any fighter squadron, although it's probably a little more spartan and is lined with the ubiquitous flying stickers.

In front of Building 201, right across I Street, is the Nellis ramp, where the Players' aircraft are parked against the backdrop of Sunrise Mountain, the most photographed mountain in aviation. North along I Street are, in order, the Fighter Weapons Schools (with two very real looking Soviet T-62 tanks in the parking lot of the A-10 FWS), the

58

64th and 65th Aggressor Squadron's headquarters (with red stars all over the outside and inside, even on—*I kid you not!*—the toilet seats in the 64th's men's room), and, across the street, the Thunderbirds' hangar, with a big scale model of their new T-Bird F–16 outside the door on a pedestal.

The flight line at Nellis is paradise for tailspotters, and keeping aviation buffs off the ramp is a full-time job for the security police. But be forewarned —any trespasser, especially some unauthorized personnel wandering around the test aircraft, is likely to find himself spread-eagled, flat on his stomach with his nose on the yellow line.

The ramp is a stirring sight, but all the action takes place up north at the ranges. We have already seen how the Red Baron report, with its detailed analysis of air-to-air training deficiencies led to the creation of the Aggressors and to Red Flag itself. But MiGs were not the only threat in Southeast Asia. Electronic warfare played a significant part in the Vietnam air war. For the first time, American pilots faced radar-directed, surface-to-air missiles and antiaircraft artillery. In this, too, their training was found lacking.

As far back as 1967, a group of visionary Air Force colonels had proposed "Facility X," an electronic warfare testing and training range. But the Air Force wasn't ready to invest the money and effort, and Facility X was never built. The concept returned with the Red Baron report, and Facility X became the Continental Operations Range (COR), a very ambitious project that would have linked weapons ranges across the United States into a unified electronic warfare and bombing range.

"Right after Southeast Asia we decided that we needed something like what we've got up there now, where we could have a war like Red Flag," says the DO of the Nellis range group.

Continental Operations Range was the first attempt to do that, but it was a little bit overambitious. We couldn't afford all the airspace, all the *money. It was too big a bite all at once. But eventually, I think we're going to get there.*

Although the COR project might have been too ambitious, the lessons learned in its first mission, supporting the $20 million Electronic Warfare Joint Test in 1972, proved that electronic warfare *could* be realistically simulated. (Up to then, aircrews had seen hostile strobes for the first time only in simulators or, worse, in actual combat.) More importantly, the tests showed that electronic warfare training significantly improved not only survivability but aircrew performance, as well. Effective EW training was becoming a necessity.

"When they had the '73 war," says the range group DO, "when Egypt and Israel went at it for those two weeks, we convinced ourselves once more that we had to be able to simulate the enemy's integrated air defense system and to learn how to defeat it or work around it, or we just weren't going to win. That's all there was to it."

In 1976 the range group was given the authority to reserve land and buy equipment to stock the ranges with simulated threats and targets. The Tactical Fighter Weapons Center Range Group is comprised of three ranges—Tonopah Electronic Warfare Range, Caliente Electronic Warfare Range, and Tolicha Peak Electronic Warfare Range—a total of three million acres, all between 100 and 250 miles northeast of Nellis AFB.

The Nellis range is used for many other missions besides Red Flag, including training for the 474th TFW (the F–16 wing based at Nellis), the Fighter Weapons School, the Aggressor's in-house training, Navy and Marine Corps training, USAF operational test and evaluation, and even cruise missile survivability training. The responsibility for coordinating and monitoring all the various range users falls upon the Range Control Center (RCC).

The RCC uses inputs from three FAA radars (Cedar City, Tonopah, and Angel's Peak) to display, in full color and great detail, the range activity on the "Big Board." The Big Board is just that—a huge monitor the size of a movie screen that occupies a wall in "Blackjack," the RCC master control room. The Big Board uses IFF (Identification, Friend or Foe) squawks and radar returns to paint a picture of what every aircraft on the range is up to: altitude, designated mission, and a ninety-second history of where it's been, as well as which radar threats are turned on, and what they're looking at. "It's a big Atari set, is what it is," says one radar control officer.

The RCC is the headquarters of the White Forces, Red Flag referees, charged with making sure the Players don't stray out-of-bounds and that no unauthorized aircraft enter the area where the battle is taking place. "There's always the Big Sky theory," says a range officer. "But when you've got some turkey in a single-engine Cessna in the middle of a bunch of people playing real, supersonic war, the little guy causes quite a problem."

The White Force knows where everyone is because the Players are "squawking IFF," broadcasting their identity through the use of Identification, Friend or Foe transponders. But the RCC controllers are careful not to give the different forces any more information than they would normally have in real battle.

"When the real war starts, we ain't gonna squawk for them, and they ain't gonna squawk for us," says a Nellis radar officer. "Besides, you don't want to make the enemy look ten feet tall if he really isn't."

"We have pretty strict rules on the use of IFF, what you can do with it and what you can't," says the Red Flag commander.

We've usually got a rule of engagement, which is not unlike war, that says you can't shoot unless you've positively identified the guy. You don't want to shoot an airliner coming out of Prague full of babies or something.

The Blue Force, for example, gets almost all its "scope dope" from the AWACS. They are allowed

The "control tower" at dry Texas Lake landing area.

to interrogate aircraft using IFF mode 1 or 2, more secure wartime modes, as opposed to mode 3, which the FAA uses.

The Red Force is controlled by Aggressor GCI controllers using a Soviet-style radar set at "Battalion Headquarters" underneath the Blackjack control room. In an emergency, of course, Blackjack takes over.

The Nellis range is often described as being almost the size of Switzerland. Technically it is, since it has more than ten million acres of controlled airspace. But about 70 percent of that is Military Operation Area (MOA). The Players can fly supersonically in an MOA, between 100 and 50,000 feet, but they can't drop bombs there. So the Nellis MOAs west of the 115th meridian, Caliente West and East, Cedar and Elgin North and South, are "no-play" areas where the Red Forces are not allowed to enter. The Blue Forces use the eastern MOAs to set up their tanker tracks and as an assembly area. After they take off from Nellis, the Players usually turn northwest at Fossil Ridge, head up the "Sally Corridor" in an instrument departure, and join up over Texas Lake, a dry lake bed in Caliente West once used as an emergency landing strip for X-15 flights, and, more recently, as a forward base for A-10 operations during a recent Red Flag exercise. After all the aircraft in the mission package have sorted themselves out, they "push the Gap," and the fight's on.

Coyote North, the first hostile area the Players enter, has been the scene of some terrific air battles. The Aggressors have even been known to "CAP the Gap," maintain a combat air patrol directly above Student Gap, the entrance to the target area.

Red Flag participants are keen on "geo-refs" (geographic references) primarily because so much of the country out on the range looks the same. In Coyote North, most of the geo-refs are

Nellis Bombing and Gunnery Range

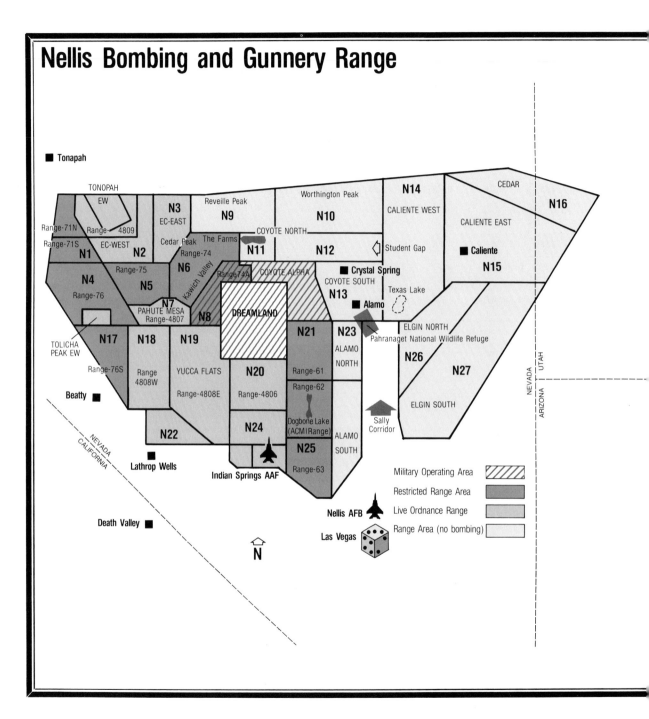

■ Tonapah

TONOPAH

EW

Range-71N Range-4809

Range-71S EC-WEST

N1

N3
EC-EAST

N9 Reveille Peak

N10 Worthington Peak

N14

CEDAR

N16

CALIENTE WEST

CALIENTE EAST

Cedar Peak The Farms COYOTE NORTH

N2 Range-74 N11 N12 ◇ Student Gap

N6 Range-75

Range74A COYOTE ALPHA ■ Crystal Spring

N4 COYOTE SOUTH

N5 COYOTE SOUTH

Range-76 N13 ■ Caliente

N15

N7 N8 DREAMLAND ■ Alamo Texas Lake

PAHUTE MESA Range-4807

TOLICHA PEAK EW N17 N18 N19 N21 N23 ELGIN NORTH

Pahranaget National Wildlife Refuge

ALAMO NORTH N26

Range-76S N20 Range-61 N27

Range 4808W

YUCCA FLATS Range-62 ELGIN SOUTH

Beatty ■ Range-4808E Range-4806 Dogbone Lake (ACMI Range)

Sally Corridor

N22 N24 ALAMO SOUTH

Lathrop Wells ■ N25

Indian Springs AAF Range-63

Death Valley ■

NEVADA / CALIFORNIA

NEVADA / UTAH

ARIZONA / UTAH

⇧ N

Nellis AFB ✈

Las Vegas 🎲

Military Operating Area ▨

Restricted Range Area ▬

Live Ordnance Range ▬

Range Area (no bombing) ▭

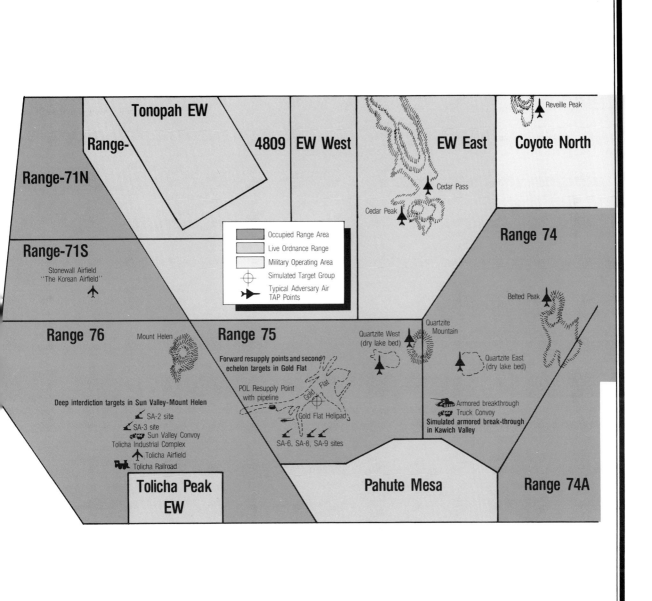

Tonopah EW

Range-

Range-71N

4809   EW West   EW East   Coyote North

Reveille Peak

Cedar Pass

Cedar Peak

Range-71S

Stonewall Airfield
"The Korean Airfield"

Range 74

Occupied Range Area
Live Ordnance Range
Military Operating Area
Simulated Target Group
Typical Adversary Air
TAP Points

Belted Peak

Range 76

Mount Helen

Range 75

Quartzite West
(dry lake bed)

Quartzite
Mountain

Forward resupply points and second
echelon targets in Gold Flat

Quartzite East
(dry lake bed)

POL Resupply Point
with pipeline

Gold Flat

Gold Flat Helipad

Deep interdiction targets in Sun Valley-Mount Helen

SA-2 site
SA-3 site
Sun Valley Convoy
Tolicha Industrial Complex
Tolicha Airfield
Tolicha Railroad

SA-6, SA-8, SA-9 sites

Armored breakthrough
Truck Convoy
Simulated armored break-through
in Kawich Valley

Tolicha Peak
EW

Pahute Mesa

Range 74A

"Smoky SAM" rocket simulates smoke trail of ground-launched antiaircraft missile.

mountains: Mount Irish and Coyote Peak to the south, and Worthington and Reveille Peak up north. Worthington, sometimes called "the Dinosaur," is an especially significant spot for Blue air-to-air pilots, as it is usually their "regeneration point"—"home base" where "shot down" fighters must tag up before they come back to life. CAPing the enemy's regeneration points is frowned upon, but is often done, nonetheless.

Since Coyote is not a range but a Military Operating Area, there are spots the Players must be careful not to overfly too low or too fast. North of

the Sally Corridor is the Pahranagat National Wildlife Refuge, and the "towns" of Alamo and Crystal Springs, usually nothing more than a couple of ranches and a post office. More in the way, at the western part of Coyote North near the entrance to the ranges, are "the Farms," green discs of irrigated land that stand out prominently against the perpetually brown desert ("It's about the only thing that's growing out there," says one pilot), and Rachel, a town too small to be on the map, but not too small to complain about sonic booms rattling the windows of the mobile homes.

Actual live bombing is done only on the numbered ranges—dropping live ordnance on the live citizens underneath the Military Operating Areas or on the Dreamland Munchkins is *not done.* The ranges that have a name—EC East and EC West, Tolicha Peak EW, and Pahute Mesa—also have people in them, so no bombing allowed there either. And there are some *numbered* ranges that are not used at Red Flag. The "Sixty-series" ranges (R-61, R-62, and R-63, west of the Sally Corridor and near Indian Springs Auxiliary Airfield) are used mainly by the 474th TFW, the Fighter Weapons School, and for operation test and evaluation of new equipment. R-62 is the site of the Nellis Air Combat Maneuvering Instrumentation range at Dogbone Lake, where the now infamous AIMVAL/ACEVAL tests took place.

This leaves the "Seventy-series" ranges, and this is where all the air-to-ground action takes place at Red Flag. There are more than fifty different types of targets scattered through R-71, R-74, R-75, and R-76: tanks, trucks, SAMs, AAA, airfields, helipads, industrial areas, bridges, radar sites, rail yards, trains, tunnels, pipelines—it goes on and on.

The ranges can be used separately, but in Red Flag they are grouped together to simulate the invasion of a friendly country by a neighboring, hostile nation. The targets are placed accordingly, so as the Players fly east to west, they are met with threats and targets associated with, respectively, the FEBA (Forward Edge of Battle Area), the second echelon, and the enemy's homeland.

The easternmost range, R-74, is a "light ordnance target area." (To USAF, which doesn't know the meaning of the word excessive, "light ordnance" means any bomb weighing fewer than 3,000 pounds.) This is where they put any target they don't want bombed into oblivion, so this is where to look for the march of the 200 Soviet tanks and armored vehicles, simulating a mechanized breakthrough. (The tanks are either real or made of plywood or polystyrene, and might be manufactured by a contractor, USAF personnel at Indian Springs, or Soviet workers, depending upon whom one asks.) R-74 is A-10 country, the easternmost edge of the FLOT (Forward Line of Troops), where the Warthogs live and work. It is also a spot to keep a good lookout for "Smokey SAM."

Smokey SAM is a nasty little rocket made of styrofoam and a cardboard paper-towel tube full of propellant. It was developed at the China Lake Naval Weapons Center after Red Flag pilots complained that the video cameras simulating Soviet infrared missile system sites had an unfair advantage. After all, the pilots *would* have taken evasive action if the sites had launched a smoking, flaming missile at them, just like the real bad guys would— but how could they avoid something they couldn't see?

Well, they can see Smokey SAM, with its 1,000 feet of billowing white smoke. The little suckers are launched from modified model rocket electric launchers. They aren't pointed *at* anyone, just up. But the Smokey SAMs are said to have been a real shot in the arm to the laundry business at Nellis, and the cleaners can't wait until next year when the flak simulators hit the ranges.

Farther back is R-75, where most of the newer, mobile, "high-threat" SAMs lurk, the SA-6s, SA-8s, and whatever other Black Trash the Soviets have dreamed up to protect the FEBA and the second echelon. There is also a helipad, a forward airfield, and a POL (Petroleum, Oil, and Lubrication) dump, complete with pipeline (actually just telephone poles painted white and laid end to end).

R-75 is also a good place to look for guns: in this case the "T-3" radars, simulating the gun laying systems for antiaircraft artillery 57mm or larger, and the unlikely marriage of the M-114 scout vehicle and the radar from an F-5, simulating the Soviet ZSU-23-4. The lightly armored M-114 never caught on with the Army, and the F-5's radar is not exactly state of the art, but together they do a pretty good impression of the four-barrelled "Shilka" antiaircraft vehicle and its Gun Dish radar. At least it's mobile, unlike most of the other simulated threat radar systems out on the range. Well, semimobile, anyway.

"We can't just run around the desert out there," says a range officer.

We have to load them up on flatbed trucks and move them on the roads. I don't think it's unrealistic that they [environmental agencies] control us. We've got eight out there now and fourteen more coming in. If they let us just go hog-wild out there, we could tear up a lot of desert.

Like the fake Shilkas, the rest of the electronic equipment out on the range is Made in America; the U.S. Air Force says there is *no* Soviet manufactured equipment used in Red Flag, despite what you might have read. The radars may use the same frequencies, pulse widths, and scan patterns as the "Low Blow," "Fan Song," "Straight Flush," and the rest of the Soviet radars NATO assigns funny names to, but they are either built from scratch under contract or, more often, are existing radar systems heavily modified. As such, they sometimes might not look much like their Soviet counterparts, but a range officer says that's no big deal:

The Army has a thing called an XMO8, which is a pretty cotton-pickin' accurate reproduction of an

SA-8. They need that visual cue for their helicopter pilots. But it's very expensive to reproduce these things visually, and we don't need that visual cue in the Air Force. The big thing we're after is the antenna sail pattern, so that we get the same lobes and side lobes and the same frequencies and power, so that when the guy sees it on his RHAW [Radar Homing and Warning] gear in his airplane, the same light is lit up as the thing this thing is simulating.

Besides, the pilots never see the actual radar emitters on the range, and thereby hangs a tale. Even though the range threat radar operators sometimes scrawl big red stars on their control

Dummy SAM installations on the Nellis range. Electronic emissions emanate from nearby threat radars.

vans, the radar equipment is always tucked safely away in EC West and East, Pahute Mesa, and Tolicha Peak EW. Sure, the "ZSU-23-4" drivers often park right across the border from the numbered ranges, but they must always stay at least five miles away from the live ordnance target area.

This is quite understandable, but sometimes confusing for the pilots. Wild Weasel jocks routinely develop "Red Flag Schizophrenia" when they can clearly see the simulated target under

Armored vehicles and trucks, ravaged by repeated bomb and gun attacks, dot the Red Flag landscape.

their port wing, but the *emissions* from that simulated target are coming from a place ten miles to their right. This is especially frustrating when they are tasked to "destroy" the site with an antiradiation missile, because there are no radar emissions coming from the target to home in on.

Enter the "nitnoi," an omnidirectional, unmanned threat emitter. "Nitnoi" is a word of Southeast Asian origin, meaning "no big thing." In this case, nitnois are radar antennas stuck right on top of the targets they're simulating, linked by a microwave relay to the manned radar station, so pilots can follow the radar beams right down to the simulated targets. The bad news is that it's going to be a couple of years before nitnois sprout up on the range.

"We are remoting, as part of the range improvement program," says a Red Flag officer.

Of course, that's always a budget issue, to the extent that we can invest in non-wartime equipment. We will be gradually filling in those target areas with remoted threat emitters that will be hardened to minimize the chance of their destruction, yet will be relatively low dollar cost, so that if

we actually hit the antenna, then we just go out, put a new one up, and go on with the war.

"Non-wartime equipment" presumably includes the targets themselves, and the U.S. Air Force can't justify spending any more than they have to in constructing precise replicas of objects they're just going to pound back into the desert floor anyway.

"Now, when a guy's coming along at 500 knots and 500 feet, those tanks look pretty realistic. But looking at them a little closer, you can see they're really just plywood replicas," says a Nellis range officer.

The fighter pilot doesn't care whether it's got an engine, or wheels, or whatever, as long as it's that shape and size.

C-130 drivers traverse Red Flag range at 300-feet altitude prior to rapid descent onto Texas Lake.

Besides, it costs quite a bit to re-equip an entire Motorized Rifle Division, even if it is made out of plywood and imagination.

"It's very expensive to put these targets out there," says a Red Flag staff officer.

I couldn't even give you a wag at how much they cost. But every exercise, every two-week period —actually, every day, almost—some of the mock-up targets get totally obliterated so they have to be rebuilt.

But visitors to Red Flag, who have read all about the range targets, are always disappointed when confronted with the real thing. This is especially

Big C-130 Hercules must attempt to evade Red Force fighters during Texas Lake resupply missions.

true in R-76, the enemy's "rear area," where the targets normally associated with deep interdiction are located. In the eastern ranges, the plywood and plastic tanks look pretty good, and the surplus Army tracked vehicles with surplus missiles do a creditable impersonation of Soviet mobile SAMs defending the POL dump and helipad in Gold Flat. But in R-76, the "Industrial Complex, complete with train and ten miles of track leading to a mountain tunnel" turns out to be less impressive. "Tolicha Peak Industrial Complex" is actually little more than frames of old buildings and debris from other destroyed targets slung together two stories high with baling wire. The train is another monument to Spot-Weld; the engine is made of more junk, and behind it trails a series of derelict, porta-

ble, maintenance shelters. The track is just a ten-mile scar scratched on the desert, and the tunnel, a hole in the side of a mountain, is closed every time the F-16s are unleashed upon it. It looks real enough to busy fighter jocks with blurred eyeballs, and the targets are a tribute to the ingenuity of the range personnel, but anyone expecting Tolicha Peak Industrial Complex to resemble Pittsburgh is going to be disappointed.

The airfields are a little more convincing. True, the runways and taxiways are still scratched out on the desert, but at least they've got real planes. The target aircraft—usually F-84s and F-86s—

Simulated enemy airfield is laid out on Red Flag range with SAM defenses.

are rescued from the USAF "Boneyard" at Davis-Monthan AFB, Arizona, and hauled out to the range on flatbed trailers. There are two deep interdiction airfields: Tolicha Airfield in R–76, constructed along the lines of eastern European air bases; and Stonewall Airfield, sometimes called the "Korean Airfield," in R–71.

Like most of the high-value targets in R–76, Tolicha Airfield is set up for the television optical scoring system (TOSS). Although there is no "score" in Red Flag, the aircrews want to know whether or not their bombs hit the target, and they find that out with TOSS.

They also find out, at the mass briefing held after every mission, if they were "shot down" by antiaircraft guns or SAMs. The video cameras and the "Smokey SAMs" give the pilots a pretty good idea of whether or not they were tracked by infrared missiles. And with radar-directed SAMs, the tech-

nicians at Blackjack can almost look over the shoulders of the threat operators out on the range. They could pass a real-time SAM kill on the Players, if they wanted.

But they don't want to give that information on the air; you never know who's listening to the radio, and the Air Force doesn't want to let the bad guys know what they're doing wrong—or right. RCC is working on a secure data link that will let the pilots know when they're shot down by a SAM without broadcasting it over the radio. And when that's in place, real-time SAM kill removal for the players will probably be the rule, especially during the later missions.

A system like the ACMI would be a real benefit to the Red Flag participants. On landing, they

70

could be given a minute by minute computer read-out of the mission they've just flown, including all their aircraft parameters, their mission results, and all attacks made against them. The Air Force is looking hard at installing a Time Space Position Indicator (TSPI) over the Nellis ranges for use in Red Flag. (The Cubic Corporation's ACMI is just a form of TSPI, like the Global Positioning Satellite or RMS–2, General Dynamics' Range Measurement System.)

"I'd like to have it," says the Red Flag CO. "Not so I can manage the war, but so I can record it and give it back to the aircrew and say, 'Here's a picture of exactly what happened.'"

No one denies that TSPI is a natural for a program like Red Flag, as well as for all the other users of the Nellis ranges, but the problem, again, is "non-wartime equipment." Any TSPI system would be frightfully expensive, so it's a big deci-

Korean war-era F-84s are trucked from Davis-Monthan AFB graveyard to serve as realistic airfield targets.

sion. But they could use it out on the range. There's a saying in the Air Force: "You can always tell a fighter pilot, but you can't tell him much."

Still, the Nellis range is a great place to throw a war, a vast improvement over the cramped, unrealistic, bombing targets the squadrons are used to. Even with its restrictions, pilots look forward to visiting the range, to returning like swallows to Gold Flat and Kawich Valley, to Cedar Peak and Cedar Pass, to Quartzite Mountain and Belted Peak and Mount Helen and all the other geo-refs fought over so fiercely at every Red Flag.

"It's a lot bigger than what we're used to," says one Eagle pilot. "And it's great training. But it could always be better."

Chapter 4
The Edge of the Envelope

For cheerful invincibility, for maximum martial correctness, for sheer "Samurai presence," it's hard to beat a USAF fighter pilot in full combat drag. He radiates confidence and competence, filling whatever space he inhabits with the gentle rustling of the modern technological warrior. The jangling and jostling of the jacks, hoses, cables, stays, buckles, and curraises that plug him into his jet (and it to him!) tinkle out a lullaby that sings, "Sleep tight, America, Daddy's got the CAP."

If you ask him he will tell you (after a picosecond's worth of modesty, a quality that only *bad* fighter pilots are good at anyway): Hell, yes, he's the best there is, a real air-to-air dragon and everybody else better keep out of his sky. The Air Force likes this attitude—trains for it, in fact—because anyone with the merest doubt in his ability has no business strapping on one of their $20 million, computer-driven, Mach II, titanium, shark-mouthed jets anyway.

But the truth is, our young pilot doesn't know how good he is. Nobody does, not even the Air Force, who would certainly like to be able to pick out the aces-of-the-bases, the real killers-of-the-sky, from the Dilberts and the Weak Dicks before the difference becomes important. The new guy may be bright and brave, a good stick-and-rudder

---

A Nellis-based F–16 approaches the field. An F–16 wing, the 474th, is one of the many units operating independently of Red Flag at the huge base.

---

man with the greatest pair of hands since Luke Skywalker. But that doesn't mean he's a good combat pilot, that he'll be able to do the job or even return from his first mission.

Right after the Vietnam War, *Time* magazine did a story on a Marine fighter squadron and came up with what may sound like an odd quote: "The common denominator of the guys here is that we all love to fly," said a Marine fighter jock. "But the sad truth is, in terms of quantity and quality, you do your best flying in wartime."

This doesn't mean fighter jocks pray for war. But that Marine A–4 driver had the guts to say what everyone in the fighter community has known all along: there is nothing like actual combat to train fighter pilots. People say aces are born and not made, and maybe that's true. But you *can* make survivors. It's easy. You make survivors the same way you make diamonds—pressure, and lots of it.

War is hell. It is an awful mess, the most counterproductive activity human beings can engage in. Nobody knows the horrors of war more than the professionals our society hires to do its fighting for it. To them, there's only one thing worse than going to war, and that's going to war unprepared.

Strange things happen in wartime. People and machines are shoved to the edge with no room for error. Combat always increases the number of aircraft accidents: planes running into one another, either in dogfights or just flying in formation; planes crashing into the ground trying to evade radar coverage; planes departing controlled flight

from dangerous maneuvers. These crashes are not considered combat losses, but that's exactly what they are—industrial accidents inherent in the war business, the result of fear, aggression, the killer instinct, the survival instinct. Whatever you call it, it's the quality that will forever separate peacetime training from the real thing.

Aircraft are said to have an "envelope," the limits of their performance in terms of speed and altitude. The safest area is the heart of the envelope, where there is room for error. But in order to survive and be effective, pilots must fly their aircraft to the edge of the envelope, go just a little faster, or slower, or higher, or lower than the other guy. It's dangerous territory, but it's where the winners live.

An F-15 Eagle of the Fighter Weapons School taxis past the Red Flag portion of the immense Nellis ramp.

Pilots have an envelope, too. There are limits to their abilities. Pilots need to know when they are flying on the edge of their personal envelope, and the trouble with most peacetime training is that they are not allowed to find out. This is understandable; training is a trade-off. There's no use in killing off pilots just to find the areas where they needed more training. But the objection pilots have traditionally had about air combat training is that in wartime they are going to be pushed to the edges of their particular envelope. And they'd prefer to find out where that is without someone shooting at them.

USAF air-to-air training in the early stages of the Vietnam War was inadequate, for just this reason. The pilots were all well-trained aviators, but their preparation as warriors was not up to the demands of modern air combat. The Red Baron study pointed out the need for more realistic air warfare training, but this was not news to most Air Force pilots. What the Red Baron study and the war in Southeast Asia did was send a signal to USAF brass that the trade-off between safety and realistic training was out of balance, that the lives saved through coddling training programs were not equal to the lives lost through inadequate preparation for war. It was a hard decision, a real life-and-death decision, but the USAF decided to embark on a realistic air combat training program.

Holloman F-15 driver trades cowboy hat for his helmet as he arrives at Nellis for Red Flag 82-5.

The planners realized it was going to be a dangerous proposition, especially at first. Dissimilar air combat training (DACT)—where aircraft of different types go at it under conditions as close to actual combat as possible—was, up to that time, very restricted or nonexistent precisely because it *was* considered so dangerous. Until safe rules for DACT could be worked out, until the majority of USAF pilots got used to the idea, accidents were bound to happen. But the USAF figured the accident rate would come down over time.

As it turns out, that's exactly what happened. The original DACT rules, as worked out for the

Aggressors and at the Navy's Top Gun program, were adapted for Red Flag and expanded.

The first Red Flags were truly red. There were even some murmurs of canceling the program if the accident rate didn't come down. (Top Gun had gone through the same thing years before.) In all, thirty-three aircrew members have died and thirty-four aircraft have been destroyed at Red Flag since its introduction in 1975. Most of these accidents took place in the early years of the program. Pilots say that although the first Red Flags may not have been more realistic, they were certainly more *sporting*. But as the program has matured the accident rate has declined, even though there are more aircraft and more missions at Red Flag now than ever before.

"Four of those thirty-four [Red Flag losses] hit the ground doing poor pop-up maneuvers," says the Red Flag CO.

Three hit the ground evading the video threat [the TV recorders simulating optically guided anti-aircraft threats]. *We know that because we've got the video. Twenty-three of them flew their airplanes into the ground. That makes me real mad — wrong set of priorities.*

I tell the pilots their first priority threat out here has two subcategories and it'll kill them both times: running into another airplane and hitting the ground. Now that's number one priority for everything they do out here, recognizing that the biggest threat in this Redland territory out here is the ground or hitting another airplane. And if they ever get priority number two, three, four, five, or six confused with number one, they'll probably get sent home in a bag. It is still simulated *war, and there is nothing at Nellis worth dying for.*

Red Flag is always going to be dangerous, by its very nature. But USAF planners have learned from experience and have formulated a set of rules that seems to balance realism and safety. There are some pilots who say the rules don't go far enough, that they are still far from wartime conditions.

That's true. In any safety versus realism issue, the Air Force will always come down on the side of safety. But these DACT guidelines (called Rules of Engagement or ROE) are far more realistic than the pre-Vietnam "flagpole missions," and every pilot welcomes the change.

This list has been garnered from different sources and is meant only to represent a typical ROE. The comments following each particular rule concern the rationale behind it and its relationship to actual combat:

1. Insure:

A. All pilots will not be scheduled for sorties, maneuvers beyond their ability.

Each squadron's "ops shop," the squadron office responsible for scheduling and planning missions, monitors the proficiency of each pilot to make sure he is getting enough of the right kind of training to keep "mission-ready" (MR). The wing's Stan-Eval (Standards and Evaluation) officers give the squadron jocks "check-rides" to make certain the pilot and his training are up to the Air Force standards.

In terms of Red Flag, this means it's important that the pilots are authorized to fly the type of missions they will be ordered to fly over the Nellis ranges. Red Flag is no place for check-rides and cram courses, and pilots who are not mission-ready might as well stay home. For example, during the first week of the two-week Red Flag war, *no* pilot is allowed to fly below 300 feet on the ranges. However, in the second week, the jocks are permitted to fly as low as 100 feet above ground level, *provided* their commanding officer writes a letter to the Red Flag and 57th TFTW commanders, saying they have been checked out and cleared to go that low, according to standard USAF step-down training guidelines. (During the second week, the Players are also often allowed to compress their times-over-target.) A hundred feet is still not as low as some air-to-ground pilots

Navy F-14 Tomcats "Cap the Gap" on the side of the Red Force.

say they'll fly in wartime, but it's still very dangerous, and Red Flag is no place to be shaving the rocks and parting the sand for the first time.

B. Mission will be briefed IAW, TACR, 51-2 if DAC sortie.

These are routine USAF regulations and guidelines and standard dissimilar air combat rules of engagement. As one jock has written, "These rules have not been formulated as just another step in the aircrew harassment program, but have been developed as common sense guidelines to insure the safe conduct of the mission." That is, they are the best compromise so far between realism and safety, and are common not only throughout the Air Force, but are similar to U.S. Navy and Marine DACT rules as well.

2. Rules of Engagement:

A. The Defender must assume an aircraft chasing him into the sun has lost visual contact and he is responsible for maintaining separation.

There are two problems with this particular rule: the first is, it doesn't make much sense in terms of combat realism. Since the days of the Red Baron, pilots have used the sun to hide in while attacking and defending, primarily because the glare makes it difficult to pick out an aircraft silhouetted against the sun. Also, with heat-seeking missiles, defenders often use the sun's heat to distract the infrared seeker heads in most air-to-air missiles. In close-in

combat with F–15s and F–16s, the Aggressors often have no other choice but to take the attacker into the sun and hope he'll lose his visual contact in the glare.

The second problem with the rule is that it makes the defender responsible for maintaining separation. This makes sense, because the whole point of taking an attacker into the sun is to try to make him lose sight of the defender anyway. But the defender doesn't always know when the attacker has lost visual contact, and, in the case of F–4s and F–5s with limited rearward vision, the *defender* doesn't always have a visual on the attacker. Also, it's quite possible to take someone into the sun and not even know it. So in most cases now, the rule is that the defender going into the sun must maintain a "predictable" flight path, and if the attacker loses visual contact he will clear to the right.

B. If visual contact is lost during setups for engagements, the flight leader will assure that altitude separation is provided until Tally-ho.

This is part of the "contract," an agreement between the pilots, either briefed before the flight or understood from long experience of flying together. It's important that safe separation altitudes be briefed beforehand, because for the rule to take effect, obviously, the opponents can't see each other; neither one knows at that moment what a safe separation altitude is. The problem gets stickier when the two sides are operating on different radio frequencies. This enhances realism, but introduces a time lag between the moment the no-visual call is made and when it is passed.

C. If two aircraft approach head-on, each fighter will clear to the right and the fighter with the higher nose position will attempt to go above the opponent.

This is often paraphrased as "nose-high goes high." The most dangerous situation develops when two turning aircraft meet head-on (for example, an aircraft turning left meets an aircraft turning right at the bottom of the "horseshoe") because the reaction time is cut drastically short. But the rule still applies.

D. Front quarter gun attacks are not authorized.

This is another example where realism has been sacrificed for safety. And rightly so. With closing speeds of Mach II possible, or even probable, the Nellis range is no place to play chicken. But in wartime, *most* of the cannon attacks would be made against the front quarter. This is especially true with aircraft like the F–4, where the pilot, usually fighting against an aircraft that turns better than his Phantom, wants to pass as closely as possible to the bandit to prevent it from gaining enough room to turn and convert on the F–4's six o'clock. The Soviets are also fond of head-on gun attacks (which they call *Lobovaya Ataka*). Their aircraft usually carry heavier gun-armament than American fighters, but the slow-firing Soviet cannon is much more useful in front-quarter attacks than from any other quadrant because of the longer exposure time.

Some front-quarter gun attacks are allowed at Red Flag. A–10 drivers, who must depend solely on their massive 30mm GAU–8A cannon for air-to-air protection, are cleared for front-quarter gun attacks, but even they must break off at 1,000 feet.

As new weapons systems come along, the rules have to be changed to accommodate their enhanced performance. Right now, it's the new generation of "magic missiles"—in this case, the latest version of the Sidewinder, the AIM–9L—that is causing problems for ROE writers. With its expanded envelope and all-angle, all-aspect capability, the "Lima" can now be used in some ranges

A Blue Force F-16 wriggles in the pipper of an Aggressor F-5 as the 16mm gun camera records the encounter.

and angles that were formerly possible only with air-to-air cannons. So AIM–9L shots on the front quarter are allowed only to a minimum range of 9,000 feet at Red Flag, although the missile's actual minimum range is much closer.

E. All rear-quarter attacks will be initiated against the trailing wingman in an element. Attacks may be initiated against any element.

The reasoning behind this is that a fighter trying to get behind the lead aircraft runs the risk of a midair collision with the bandit's wingman coming up from the rear. It's a sound move tactically, too, because the Soviets always travel in pairs, although often with such vast horizontal or altitudinal separation that it's difficult to pick up the trailer—that's the idea. The Red Baron always attacked the trailer, not only because that was a good way not to be sandwiched, but also because the trailer was usually the less experienced pilot.

On the other hand, if the targets are separated by such distance as to make an attack on the leader possible and still have enough time and space to defend against the trailer, attacking the leader may be a good idea. "If they're separated by three or more miles," says a Red Flag briefing officer, "be my guest."

At any rate, the terminology of this rule may be a bit outdated. Air-to-air fighters hardly ever fight in two-ship elements anymore. Instead, the USAF has gone to the "Fluid Two," a two-ship formation with each aircraft effectively taking the part of each two-ship element in the old, Vietnam era "Fluid Four." Also, the notion of a "trailer" is fast becoming extinct. In a Fluid Two, the aircraft may be separated by great horizontal and vertical distances, but they will almost always be flying line-abreast. (*Nobody* wants to be the trailer these days. Trailers get killed.) However, if each aircraft

The gun sight of an Aggressor F-5 tracks an F-4 in a shallow right turn.

in the Fluid Two is considered an "element," the rule still holds true.

F. Any flight member can terminate the engagement by transmitting "knock if off," at which time all participants will cease maneuvering and acknowledge with call sign.

This rule is expanded somewhat at Red Flag, because the Red Flag war is itself so expansive. The call "terminate" will stop only one small part of the war. For instance, "Terminate the F–5s at Cedar Pass" means someone has noticed something unusual and potentially dangerous concerning the Aggressors over a particular geographic area. The pilot who has made the call gives his call sign, and the order is passed through the separate radio frequency to the F–5s over Cedar Pass. The only person who can start the battle up again is the pilot who made the call in the first place. He does this by saying, for example, "Fight's on at Cedar Pass" (*not* "Knock it on at Cedar Pass," a phrase in vogue for a while, which is now fortunately recognized as an affront not only to safety but good English as well).

To stop the entire war, the pilot calls, "Red Flag, knock it off!" This is the big one and means something terribly wrong has happened. On a Red Flag knock-it-off call, all the participants immediately stop transmitting over the radio and go to altitude to look for chutes.

G. Fighters conducting separate attacks will maintain a minimum of 1,000 feet altitude separation on any target until Tally-ho. All aircraft will have this altitude separation within ten nautical miles. Fighters may transit target beyond six nautical miles.

This is the altitude block, and, combined with 1,000 feet minimum horizontal separation, it effectively isolates every participating aircraft in a bub-

---

As the F-5 turns too sharply, the F-4 begins to fall out of his gun sight.

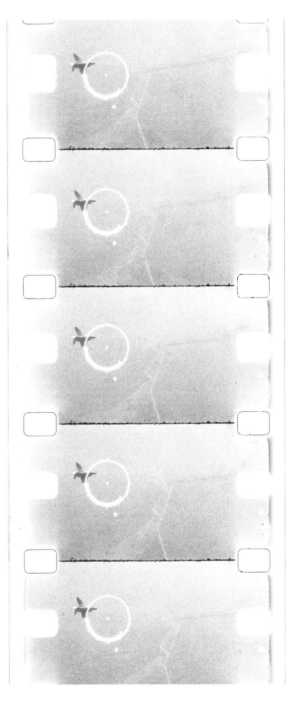

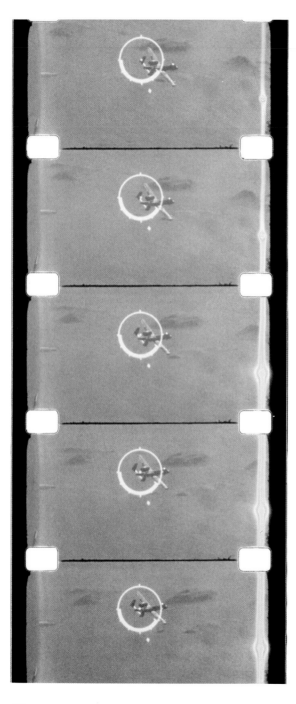

ble at least 1,000 feet in diameter. This works on paper anyway. But in the sky, in the heat of combat, it's sometimes difficult to know—or care—if a pilot is breaking someone else's "bubble." It's a good rule, but difficult to enforce, especially since the pilots involved are the only ones who know when it's broken; the fighter pilot code of honor precludes ratting on another fighter pilot (unless the other guy is a dangerous pilot, a suicidal lunatic, or a Naval aviator). Midair collisions are rare at Red Flag, but near-midair collisions are not.

Although 1,000 feet is as close as any aircraft is allowed to come to another aircraft at Red Flag, different types of aircraft have different types of "bubbles." Minimum separation for fighters, tactical airlift transports, and B-52s is 1,000 feet, but 2,000 feet is the limit for helicopters and every aircraft must keep at least 3,000 feet from the E-3A AWACS, EA-6B, and the new EF-111. (Actually, pilots probably would not want to get any closer to these last three aircraft for fear of being sterilized by their powerful microwave transmissions.)

H. Termination will be accomplished when one of the following situations occurs:
1) If the battle drifts to the border of the authorized area.

This is not as much a problem at Nellis as it might be at other bases. For one thing, even with all its restrictions, the Nellis range is still huge. And there is a Red Flag duty officer monitoring every mission by radar to insure that pilots don't wander into an area where they don't belong.

2) If an unbriefed, unscheduled flight enters the ACM work area and is a factor detrimental to the safe conduct of the mission.

Again, since the Nellis ranges are so huge and so closely monitored, the bogey—usually some poor Cessna driver, lost and frightened—is picked

---

An ungainly A-10, at a disadvantage in air combat, is directly in the bull's-eye of Aggressor guns.

up and escorted out of the Red Flag area before he becomes a danger to the participants. But it does happen.

3) If visual contact is lost by the attacking aircraft within 1 nm (nautical mile) and converging vectors exist or safe separation cannot be assured.

You'd think it would be impossible to lose sight of a fighter at a distance of a mile or less. That's what every young tiger thinks before he fights the Aggressors for the first time. Nose-on, an aircraft like the F–5 is difficult to see at any range.

In peacetime training, the procedure is to signal lost sight as well as current altitude, and turn away from the bandit's last known position. In combat this could prove fatal. This is where good radar technique comes in. A radar lock-on would at least give the pilot a clue about which section of sky to search. The F–16's radar, in particular, is adept at quick acquisition and lock-on at extremely close range.

4) When the desired learning objective is achieved.

Disengagement is always dangerous, even in training. The standard separation for DACT consists of transmitting the call sign and acknowledging the knock-it-off call, selecting military power (the highest throttle setting without using the afterburner) and climbing back to the starting altitude.

5) If stalemate occurs.

Fights without a clear, initial winner usually degenerate into slow-speed "knife fights," where nothing is learned except which pilots can fly lower and slower without losing control. This sort of slow-speed Russian roulette is called "pride maneuvers" and used to kill pilots in unauthorized "hassling" before DACT. There's no excuse for it now, and pilots have become mature enough to realize the surest way to go back to flying "flagpole missions" is to kill each other in supersonic Chicken games.

The wily Warthog driver manages to slide off the hot seat.

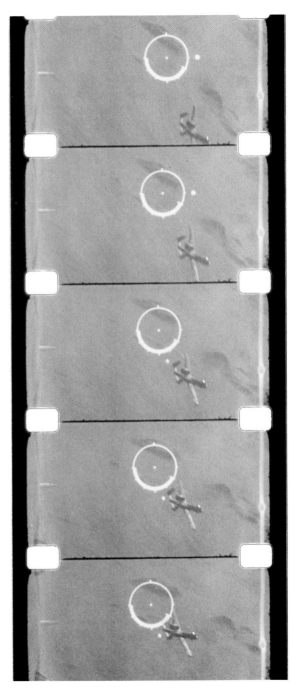

6) If any aircraft rocks its wings.

This is the universal signal for "NORDO," meaning the aircraft has lost its radio communications and is inviting another aircraft to join up on its wing to escort it back to base. Wing-rocking has been expanded at Red Flag to include all instances where a pilot, for any reason, doesn't want to fight —maybe his aircraft is low on fuel or having some other problems. The wing-rock serves to acknowledge that the pilot sees and recognizes the attacker but doesn't want to play.

7) If bingo fuel is reached.

"Bingo fuel" is the amount of fuel needed to return to base. Most fights will knock it off at "joker fuel," which is the fuel state needed to effect a valid separation. Joker fuel is much higher than bingo, because most separation maneuvers re-

The Northrop F-5E used by the Aggressors accurately simulates the Soviet MiG-21.

quire the use of afterburner, which ups fuel consumption by as much as a factor of ten. The fuel state at which the fight is called off depends on what type of training is attempted. The important thing is to be aware of the fuel state and make it a realistic part of the training scenario.

8) If a dangerous situation is developing.

This is, of course, a judgment call, so we'll let a DACT professional, a 65th Aggressor pilot, do the talking:

You can recognize from the way the guy's flying his airplane if he's exceeding the safe limits, particularly if he's flying close to the ground—that's a

big threat. *That's what we demand of these guys, to have the maturity to say "knock if off." We'll set the whole thing up again, and we'll do it right, but we'll do it within these bounds. And if somebody gets outside those bounds, we'll stop it. And we'll come down and talk to them about it afterwards.*

9) If minimum altitude or clouds are approached.

Putting minimum altitude aside for the moment, this is not a rule that helps simulate combat. Clouds, like the sun, can often be a fighter pilot's best friend—they help him hide from attackers and mask the heat from his engines to frustrate an infrared missile attack. But following another aircraft into the clouds where neither pilot can see the other is an excellent way to get killed in a mid-air collision, which is not appropriate to a peacetime training mission.

A-10s from Myrtle Beach AFB roll for an afternoon mission at Red Flag 83-5.

10) If radio failure occurs.

11) If communications deteriorate to a point that individual aircraft cannot receive all R/T (radio transmissions) pertinent to the engagement.

These two rules mean the same thing to varying degrees and point out one of the differences between regular DACT and Red Flag. Certainly in peacetime it's a good idea to quit if you can't talk to the ground, your friends, and especially your "enemy." But since Red Flag simulates war, and war these days means communications jamming, aircrew must learn to deal with it or stay home. "When we turn com-jam on, we go to roll their

85

The huge F-15 is an easy "tally" at three miles in the crystalline Nevada skies.

socks down," says a Red Flag officer. "We want them to know that when it's on, it's on." So anybody in Red Flag who gives up and goes home when his radio doesn't seem to work will be hooted out of the Nellis Officers' Club for the rest of his life.

Since Red Flag integrates both air-to-air and air-to-ground training missions in the same airspace, there are a couple of low-altitude rules added to the regular DACT ROE:

I. Attacks on aircraft below 5,000 AGL are authorized with the following limitations:
1) Attackers: The attack may commence from above or below 5,000 feet AGL and will terminate no later than minimum gun range if any member of the flight acknowledges the attack or if the attack flight begins weapons delivery (pop-up).

This is a touchy subject at Red Flag. Aircraft on final approach to ordnance delivery are always vulnerable, and at Nellis there is an additional danger because the planes are dropping live bombs. It's a delicate situation for both the strike aircraft *and* the attacker because at "minimum gun range" the attacker stands an excellent chance of being fragged by the exploding bombs or ingesting debris into the aircraft's intakes. This is why air-to-ground aircraft on final weapons delivery are left alone at Red Flag.

2) Defenders will acknowledge the attack by a radio transmission (if same frequency), a wing-rock, a level, climbing, defensive turn with a wing-rock, and return to course (as a guide, defensive turns will not exceed ninety degrees). Defenders will not maneuver counteroffensively against an attack (below 5,000 AGL).

Even though it's forbidden to attack aircraft on final weapons delivery, on the way there and back they are fair game. The Aggressors have devel-

oped a knack for loitering around the strikers and bouncing them after they complete their bombing run. This is perfectly okay, and good training for combat. Besides, in Vietnam and recent wars in the Mideast, many aircraft were shot down as they pulled up after a bombing run. It's a psychological phenomenon—the pilots, so intent on getting to the target and dropping their load in parameters, tend to let up after they let their ordnance go. And if Red Flag teaches the pilots anything, it's the virtue of paranoia.

The part about not maneuvering counteroffensively sometimes hacks the air-to-ground pilots, especially the F-16 drivers who look at bombing runs as an excuse to sucker bandits in close so they can shoot them down. But, in general, it's a good rule because there are so many aircraft at Red Flag, all loaded with live ordnance, that it's not worth the risk. In combat, of course, it's a different story.

Other missions might have a slightly different ROE, but this set of rules of engagement is pretty close to the one under which most dissimilar air combat training missions are fought.

Because Red Flag is a unique program, it has unique rules. Nowhere else are there more aircraft flying more missions at the same time, and, as one Red Flag officer puts it, "the more aircraft you have, the more rules you have." Here are some restrictions that tend to make Red Flag less than realistic in the eyes of some pilots.

First, of course, there is the Nellis range itself. It would seem, at first glance, that with 10 million acres to zoom around in, the Red Flag Players wouldn't be cramped for space.

But look again. More than half the range space is devoted to Military Operating Areas (MOAs). These are valuable slices of airspace in which fighters can zoom around supersonically above a certain level. They are nice to have (USAFE, in particular, would love to have a good-sized MOA over Germany), but still, they are restrictive. You

Above: An F-15 taxis out. *Right:* A Holloman first-timer, flying with the 8th TFS "Black Sheep."

can't drop bombs in an MOA—civilians live underneath them. So the Red Flag war can't take place there. All the Nellis-controlled MOAs are east of Student Gap, in the no-play area forbidden to adversary aircraft.

But the big kicker on the Nellis range is Dreamland (where the Department of Energy tests nuclear weapons) and the associated, restricted ranges right in the middle of the Red Flag war. It's better now than it was; Coyote Alpha used to be permanently closed to the Players. And with the air corridor from George AFB, as well as the proposed extensions of the range out to the Utah testing grounds and even down to the Army com-

pound at Fort Irwin currently being planned, the Red Flag Players will have a little more elbow room. But right now, with so much restricted airspace, there is a huge chunk of airspace taken out of the Nellis ranges.

By itself, even this limited space wouldn't be so bad. But the altitude deconfliction rule—the 1,000-foot "bubble" of airspace each aircraft is required to maintain—means the mission package going in must be careful not to get too close to the mission package coming out. They do this by

F-4G "Wild Weasel" SAM-suppression birds.

staying on their side of the "3740 line," a geographic boundary that runs from the northern border of R-74, just north of Gunderson, Mount Irish, and Student Gap. Sometimes it's "North In, South Out"; sometimes it's "South In, North Out"; but the flow, for safety reasons, is always predictable. The only other choice is deconfliction by altitude, but since most of the Players want to fly as low as they can to sneak under the radar and hide from the Aggressors, deconfliction by altitude is not a viable choice. ("It's the kind of thing you can only get away with once in a row," says an Air National Guard Phantom driver.)

Add to Dreamland and the 3740 line the restrictions that prohibit flying with live ordnance over the parts of the electronic warfare ranges where people operate the threat radars. Then it's easy to understand why pilots sometimes complain that their options are severely restricted by the Nellis ranges, that tactical innovations—touted by USAF brass as one of the main reasons for the program —are hard to come by under conditions that force them to be predictable. The rap, in short, is that, because of the range restrictions, Red Flag missions always end up "canned."

"Everything is concentrated in one little area," says a Wild Weasel pilot. "It's not spread out like a typical Soviet Motorized Rifle Division would be."

"It's the same thing day after day after day," says a Naval aviator flying with the Red forces. "There's no flexibility in getting to the targets."

"The missions end up—I won't say canned—but it's kind of predictable in that you've only got a certain airspace up there that you can run in," says an Aggressor pilot.

You have the targets here, you've got the entry point here, and there's a little corridor that everybody has to go through in order to get there.

The Red Flag commander says he agrees, but it's all right:

It gets small in a hurry. There are airplanes everywhere all the time. That's good—I want the war to happen.

And he says even the range restrictions are, in a sense, realistic:

This is just a little bitty slice of a big war. In wartime you're going to have a zone that you're cleared into, because there's going to be zones on your left and right where other aircraft are working, where other battles are being fought. So there are divisions that are required to keep the forces separate from one another. This is just one little zone of conflict, and the fact that we have boundaries on the left and right are very realistic, because in wartime you're going to have boundaries on your left and right.

An Air National Guard pilot agrees:

I don't think the fact that the range is cramped and the bad guys always know where we're going is a valid criticism. I flew over Southeast Asia, and we had the same problem.

As in any game, there are Players at Red Flag who think the rules are slanted against them. The Blue, AFFOR (Air Force forces), aircrews complain that OPFOR (opposition forces), and the Aggressors in particular, have an unfair advantage because they know precisely where the Blue players will be and are directed under unrealistically precise ground control to the interception.

The Aggressors say it's no big deal, it's all just part of making the war happen. The F–5 is not air-refuelable, and because of the time it takes to fly all the way out to the ranges and back, they are already limited to less than twenty minutes on station. If they don't have a pretty good idea of when and where the Blue forces will be, they might as well stay at Nellis, because they don't have enough gas to go out searching.

That also has a lot to do with the GCI control. The Soviets, whom the Aggressors are trying to emulate, work very closely with the ground-based radar. The F–5's radar is just not good enough to compete on its own. Even with good GCI, the Aggressors can barely keep up with systems like the F–15.

"We don't have the systems that they have—we don't have their interface with the radar units," says a 64th Aggressor.

Our guy's working with one scope, one radar unit, and we've got to have pretty good information in order to be a threat to the Blue force. If we didn't, they wouldn't see the threat. We don't have the facilities to offer our people the same numbers they may encounter in a war.

"I'll second that," says another 64th pilot.

If we could launch sixty airplanes, we probably wouldn't need that much GCI. Launch a hundred—why not? The Israelis said Bekaa was the biggest air battle since the Battle of Britain. There were airplanes everywhere, and that's what our guys are going to see if they ever go to war.

For the most part, the guys we're fighting against want to get engaged. They're disappointed if they don't because otherwise they're not getting any training, they're just flying around out there by themselves. Even if we come in with the advantage, they'd rather do that and get engaged and find out the mistakes they can make rather than not get engaged in the first place.

For their part, the Aggressors feel there are some rules that discriminate against *them* unfairly.

Remember the "magic missiles"? Well, the AIM-9L is truly magic, no one disputes it. But the rules also consider its companion, the AIM-7F Sparrow, just as magical, and there are some hard feelings about that.

The Sparrow is a radar guided missile with a less than awesome reputation. Neither the Sparrow nor the Sidewinder had what you'd call a notable record in Southeast Asia. At one point in the war the Navy shot off fifty of them and didn't hit a damn thing. Some of those shots were out of parameters, to be sure, and after the war both missiles were improved tremendously. The latest Sidewinders have been the deciding force in both recent air wars; they transformed the Harrier from a ground attack aircraft to a real fighter in the Falklands and helped the Israelis to the best record of any air force in any war—82-to-zip—against the Syrians in the Bekaa Valley.

But the new Sparrow is still a question mark. It now has some look-down, shoot-down capability and is less likely to go scooting off into the wild blue guided only by its own bizarre electronic mentations. But it still needs to be tuned up, strobed, stroked, nudged, pointed, and urged

Left: 64th Aggressors four-ship forms up for return to Nellis. *Above:* Gomers looking for trouble over Student Gap.

along to the target. And a Sparrow shot, even in perfect parameters, is never automatic, no matter what the rules say.

"What's going to happen the first time that F-15 fires that great big AIM-7 with that big, white smoke trail?" says an Aggressor, complaining that the rules simulate the missile kill but not the telltale missile launch.

All the Soviet pilots doing their classic Soviet maneuvers—the formations are going to go to hell, I think. They're going to point at that F-15 and shoot at it. That's what I'd do if I were a Soviet pilot; I'd say, "Gah! I want to go shoot that guy!"

"There are times when I get tired of being shot down," says another Aggressor pilot.

For example, if they don't have to visually ID the aircraft, out comes the Great White Hope [the AIM-7F] and—WHOOSH!—you're a mort! And I don't see an F-15! So I go out to kill removal, turn back around, come into the fight and—WHOOSH! —another Great White Hope, and you're a mort.

So I'm turning around, doing this yo-yo dance all day until I'm a bingo fuel. I come back extremely *frustrated.*

An F–15 driver says he is not going to throw live Sparrows at the Aggressors just to give them a visual cue, but they do have rules that keep the shots honest.

You have to take into account that no missile is an "I-Wish-You-Were-Dead" missile. Sometimes it just won't work—it won't fire, or it won't guide, or it just won't get to you. So we use a two-shot kill; you have to take two shots, both of them within parameters, five seconds apart.

Sometimes, though, even with the Big Board and the videotape and HUD (Head-Up Display) cameras, it all comes down to a judgment call. Kill removal is always the most disputed part of any DACT sortie, and with so many aircraft at Red Flag, the problems are compounded.

"It's a gentlemen's agreement," says an Aggressor.

"It's a pain in the ass," says an F–15 pilot.

"I saw my kids playing cowboys and Indians," says a Red Flag staff officer.

It looked like Red Flag. You know—"You're dead!" and "No, I'm not, you're dead first!"—lots of arguing going on about who shot who first. And you just can't have that in an air-to-air engagement.

After going through a frustrating period of having too many shot-calls ignored by the "victim," Red Flag is getting tough about kill removal. Now, if the aircraft just shot down refuses to go back to the regeneration point, his whole air force—Red or Blue—will get no GCI calls of any kind passed to them. This is serious, peer group pressure, the only punishment that works on fighter pilots, so kill removal has been running a little smoother since.

But there are still so many things that just cannot be simulated. How *do* you simulate an AIM–7 launch realistically—smoke, guidance, IFF, the whole thing? And who's to say the missile can't be outmaneuvered, outrun, or spoofed by electronic countermeasures? Certainly in Real Life that sort of thing has happened time and again.

Even with these restrictions, every pilot agrees USAF air combat training has come a long way since the Vietnam War. But there are those who say it still doesn't go far enough, that the trade-off still favors safety too much at the expense of realism. They cite the words of the Navy's only Vietnam ace, Randy Cunningham: "You fight like you train." Using the training programs of other nations as examples, they say safety restrictions could provide negative training in wartime.

"The Israelis are uniformly quite good, and they take their flying very seriously," says an Aggressor pilot.

They have a charter that says, "We won't make our pilots do anything in combat they haven't practiced in peacetime." It differs from our philosophy a little bit; for example, we use altitude blocks in Red Flag. They don't use altitude blocks. They say, "Well, you're not going to use them in combat, so you're not going to use them in training." It's a little more dangerous, but a little more realistic.

His CO agrees:

The Israelis do an excellent job of training their people. They certainly have a lot of motivation when right across the street's a bad guy. But they're also not dealing with an enemy that's anywhere near as well trained as they are.

Do the Israelis have their own Aggressor squadron?

"No, they don't," he says. "They don't particularly need it."

Maybe the Israelis are a poor choice for comparison, poised, as they are, on the brink of war every day. But some pilots say there are other air forces—luckily, all allied with the United States— that have, in some respects, more no-nonsense aircrew training programs than the United States.

"I think the British training is pretty good," says another Aggressor jock.

They have a base in Gütersloh [West], Germany, and they say, "We're an occupational force, and if you don't like flying in our airspace, just keep your airliners away. We're flying VFR from ground to 20,000 feet, and if you don't like that, it's too bad; you shouldn't have lost the war."

The British pilots take their flying very seriously. American pilots take their flying very seriously, but we have a lot more constraints put on us that may or may not be artificial. Or political.

The Red Flag commander doesn't worry too much about the complaints. The program is what you make it, he says, and besides, for the new guy, the Nellis range in mock wartime is dangerous enough as it is. Red Flag is still there to give the new fighter jocks their first ten combat missions; anything else is gravy. They want to train him, not overwhelm him; put him under lots of pressure, but not bury him in it. The rules are there to keep the

British-built Jaguars of the French *Armee de l'Aire* participated in Red Flag 82–5 on the Aggressor side.

young men from dying trying, and in that respect, the Red Flag CO thinks they are finally getting the right balance:

"You always run a risk in aviation," he says of the pilots who come to Red Flag for the first time.

You want a young, aggressive man, a 22-year-old with a 40-year-old's maturity. That's asking a lot. You have to be very careful to keep the aggressiveness, because it's essential to the business, but you also have to have the maturity to recognize the limits and the value of your equipment.

So it's a fine balance—flying the airplane to the maximum capability, but not bashing it here, because you're not hurting anybody but us. It can be done. But you've got to do it safely. And you've got to fly shit hot.

Chapter 5
Players

Welcome to Redland, a mythical country perpetually ravaged by hypothetical wars. Geographically, Redland is located entirely within the borders of Nye County, Nevada. Politically it is on the other side of the world—the imaginary eighth member of the Warsaw Pact, perhaps, or some little oil-oozing nation bubbling in obscurity until war burns its name on America's Trinitrons. The U.S. Air Force says Redland is completely "notional," that no particular inference should be drawn in comparison with any real country. Well— the USAF pays the tab for Redland and can say what it wants. But Redland fits the bill for the Standard All-Purpose Hostile Country, a nation of targets and threats, which is how the military often sees the world, and rightly so.

Redland's 1,500 square miles of worthless real estate is fiercely defended by one of the most sophisticated air defense systems in the world. This is fortunate for the nonexistent Redland population, because their country declares war on, and is consistently trounced by, the U.S. Air Force five times a year—in wars that always last exactly six weeks, with campaigns that always last exactly ten days. Like America, Redland is a civilized country and never fights on weekends.

Redland—or Anastasia, Slobbovia, or Russovakia, as it is sometimes called—is a singularly

Left: Eagle on combat air patrol pounces on low-flying F–4 fighter-bombers.

unappealing place to live. It is bordered on the east by the peace-loving Blue nation; on the north by neutral Green, the Switzerland of the desert; and on the west by Stark. (God knows the USAF has dropped its share of ordnance on the English language, but occasionally it will coin a phrase of exquisite aptness. I can think of no better term for a country analogous to the Soviet Union than "Stark.") Redland's entire Gross National Product is squandered on defense. It has no cities, few roads, and a railroad that goes from nowhere to nowhere with one freight train that has never moved. Redland's national flag is a radar antenna. Its national anthem is the ominous growling that American pilots hear coming from their electronic countermeasures equipment.

The premier of Redland, the generalissimo of Slobbovia, the ruler of Russovakia's military junta is—an American major! And he rules the country, not from a heavily defended capital or presidential palace, but from a neat desk in Building 201 at Nellis Air Force Base, right down the hallway from the Red Flag commander's office! No wonder he always seems to know what the good guys are up to.

The major, of course, denies he is supreme commander of the enemy forces. He says he is merely the branch chief of the intelligence unit that creates the scenario for a realistic threat to train the aircrews and intel personnel of the squadrons that deploy to Red Flag. Sure. Next he'll be saying Redland isn't a communist country.

"For this next exercise, the country that's the 'bad guys,' is called 'Red,' " he says. "That doesn't necessarily mean communist. Just red as opposed to blue."

The old Big Lie technique! The crafty double agent says his job is to use information provided by the 4513th Adversary Threat Training Group, the master intelligence unit at Nellis, to put together a package of intelligence information. Some of it is deliberately misleading; some of it is "correct" if interpreted correctly. Added together, the information will present the friendly forces with a military and political crisis that will erupt into war a day after they arrive.

Shortly before the exercise takes place, we send out an exercise update message. In that message, we try to set the scene. We describe the geopolitical situation—how bad things are. As they arrive here, in our initial inbrief we will provide

Eighth TFS "Black Sheep" F-15s, core unit of Red Flag 82-5.

them a series of intreps, intelligence reports, indicating that the situation is worsening and we can expect hostilities by tomorrow.

At the start of the war you're going to get a lot of diplomatic reporting out of the "State Department" and military attachés. As the buildup proceeds, you're going to have reflections of the Aggressor conducting reconnaissance, both land and air, of the FEBA [Forward Edge of Battle Area].

So war comes again to Redland and everyone chooses sides. The Blue Players join AFFOR, the Air Force Forces, the good guys. Redlanders, like the Aggressors, the other adversary air Players, and the crews that operate the simulated gun, missile, and radar sites out on the range, march out and enlist in OPFOR, the opposition forces.

But the premier of Redland, the Red Flag major who thought the whole thing up in the first place, sits back and plays both sides against each other. He could tell AFFOR's intel people everything that's going to happen. But he doesn't:

We try to lead them to logical conclusions, but we don't give them all the information they need. Because you never have perfect intelligence— Never. So they have to do some very basic analysis.

But that's the way his boss, the Red Flag CO, wants it:

The intelligence people are working with my ops people as if it were a war, because we also bring a lot of young, TDY intelligence people out here who have to start thinking how you go about targeting, damage assessments, photographic intel. So they look at that flow and make the targeting decisions based on the scenario that's set up.

There is usually at least one air reconnaissance unit at every Red Flag. The intelligence personnel use the information they bring back, along with other bits and pieces gleaned from debriefs of pilots immediately after they return from their missions, to put together the next day's target list. But although they decide what should be hit, they don't try to tell the pilots how and when to hit it— that's the warlord's job.

The warlord is a position unique to Red Flag. The warlord is in charge of coordinating the various Blue forces into a cohesive unit to hit the targets he is tasked to destroy according to an Air Task Order issued three to four hours before the mission by the joint task force commander (who, strangely enough, doubles as the Red Flag CO). The warlord could be anyone from an F-15 jock to a C-130 pilot. It's not necessary for him to know all the details of how each Blue unit goes about its mission. But it *is* important that the warlord be diplomatic, and, if it comes down to it, stubborn; otherwise, some Blue units, in their natural desire to set up their missions in the most favorable con-

ditions, might put other Blue units in danger. There's a lot of horse-trading, and considerable volume sometimes, when the warlord conducts a meeting with the different mission commanders to put the day's strike together.

"It's that exchange between the various weapons systems operators that we're looking for," says the Red Flag CO.

If you're an F-111 pilot, you can fly for many years, and if you've never had the opportunity to sit and talk and plan a mission with Wild Weasels and EF-111s, with CAP, with strikers going on underneath you or close air support going on in front of you—if you've never had to talk to those guys about how they go about their business, you don't have a good understanding of what they do. And that lack of understanding is going to be a severe detriment if you go to war.

So here you have the opportunity to gain direct knowledge of how all the elements of our air force go together for maximum effectiveness. And that's one of the things about Red Flag that is not well publicized but it is essential. It's one of the two key ingredients to Red Flag: face-to-face exchange between the various weapons systems aviators. And the opportunity to fly together.

The actual plan to carry out the targeting assignments takes the form of "mission packages." A package is a composite strike force, typically consisting of, in order: recce flights, Wild Weasels and their F-15 escort (dubbed the "Wild Eagles"), the strike flights and their fighter cover, followed by more reconnaissance flights, and supported by tankers, AWACS and other electronic warfare platforms, and rescue forces.

"A package is a composite thought," says the Red Flag commander.

Each unit has a generalized purpose and a specific tasking within the overall mission itself. They'll be given a specific target and a threat briefed on that target—how it is defended and what they're supposed to do to that target.

The aircraft are assigned a mission code, a three-digit acronym that represents their assignment in the mission package. The mission code is mainly for the convenience of the range officers tracking the battle at Blackjack, where the numbers and lines representing the various flights are color-coded as to mission. Here are some typical mission codes at Red Flag:

REC (Reconnaissance)—Almost always flown by RF-4Cs, the "recce bird's" mission is tactical battlefield reconnaissance: flying over dangerous territory unarmed but very fast.

DSP (Defensive Suppression)—This means keeping the enemy SAMs and radar-directed anti-aircraft guns too busy to bother the rest of the package. DSP is the Wild Weasel's job, almost exclusively flown by F-4Gs, now that the F-105 Weasels have all been retired.

All Red Flag air activities are monitored in real time at "Blackjack," the range control center at Nellis.

OCA (Offensive Counterair)—This is airfield attack and can be flown by any strike aircraft. When Guard and Reserve A-7s come to Red Flag, they are often assigned OCA missions, where their cosmic bombing systems come in handy, and their relatively low performance is not as great a factor because they are working with other aircraft in the giant OCA mission packages.

CAS (Close Air Support)—This is the job the A-10 was built for, to clobber tanks with its huge GAU-8A 30mm cannon in support of ground troops. The A-10s work CAS with Army helicopters is a Joint Air Attack Team. More than any other USAF asset, the Warthog drivers work closely with the Army, and in some Red Flag exer-

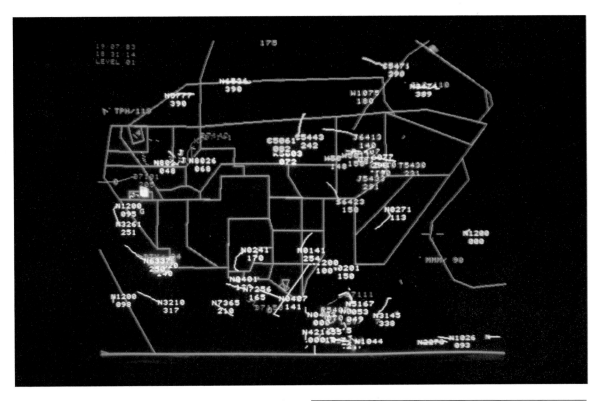

The big screen at Blackjack displays transponder codes for every aircraft over or near the Nellis range.

cises have even flown from Bicycle Lake on the Army's nearby Fort Irwin complex.

BAI (Battlefield Air Interdiction)—Another favorite A-10 mission, BAI is quite similar to CAS, but it's concerned with the second echelon of troops "ten feet past the Fire Support Coordination Line of the Army Commander."

FAC (Forward Air Control)—FAC is concerned with coordinating and targeting airstrikes and artillery fire, and is also closely tied with Army operations. In low threat areas, the USAF still might try to keep its FACs airborne. But in Europe, for example, they would probably be flying jeeps, and the OV-10 Broncos would be used mostly for relaying messages, while orbiting safely behind the lines.

INT (Interdiction)—"Going deep," interdiction is penetrating far into enemy territory to bomb sup-

ply lines, industrial complexes, and marshalling yards. This is the most complex and most typical mission package. Usually it involves all the different USAF aircraft working together. The "strike flight," the aircraft actually carrying the bombs, usually consists of F-111s or F-4s, although the F-16 has proved itself a good interdiction aircraft.

CAP (Combat Air Patrol)—This is the fighter pilot's favorite hobby, searching out and destroying enemy aircraft in dogfights. "CAP" often follows a prefix, denoting the type of combat air patrol to be flown. F-4s might fly a "LOWCAP" at low altitude, for example, and Navy fighters protecting a carrier could fly a "BARCAP," positioning themselves as a barrier between the task force and the bandits. Most often at Red Flag, the Eagles are assigned different areas to CAP at different times, and sometimes they do, but "on a blackboard a CAP is perfectly round, and we're using our radar to search," says an Eagle driver. "Well, that's a bunch of b.s.!—that's just what we use on the blackboard. The way it actually turns out is that you just roam the area at high speed, looking for anything you can."

ESA (Escort)—This is the fighter pilot's least favorite form of CAP. They don't like to be too closely tied to the strike flight and prefer to pounce on the enemy from a high, hidden perch. Note that fighters are not the only ESA aircraft; the Weasels and even the new EF-111A could fly escort missions.

ADF (Air Defense Forces)—"Bad Guy CAP"; adversary fighter operations flown by the Aggressors and other Players on the Red side.

AAR (Air-to-Air Refueling)—Tanker operations flown by SAC's KC-135s.

AWC (Airborne Warning and Control)—Radar coverage, supplied by the E-3A Sentry AWACS.

TRS (Tactical Resupply)—This is battlefield resupply by MAC's C-130s.

This last mission is a fairly recent addition, and underlines the Military Airlift Command's new emphasis on maintaining a war-ready posture. From the beginning, MAC has always been involved in the deployment of other units to Red Flag. But in the last couple of years, MAC personnel, especially the C-130 aircrews, have become Players in almost every Red Flag, and they like it.

"In the beginning, MAC was given bits and pieces of Red Flag because we were offering free airlift," says a C-130 navigator.

We would bring the troops out, MAC would pick up the tab, and they'd allow us to play. Now we're actually in every Red Flag, in every two-week period.

All the C-130s used to be in TAC until 1975, and when we went to MAC we kind of lost the realistic combat training. It is of extreme importance to us—we know that we're going to war, but we don't train totally the way we should because we don't have the opportunity. Red Flag gives us that opportunity.

So far, MAC participation as Players in Red Flag has generally been limited to C-130 operations, and about half the Hercs in each exercise come from the Air National Guard or the Air Force Reserve. MAC really gets into the Rapid Deployment Force Red Flag exercises, hauling fuel and ammo out to desert dumps.

One of the best things about MAC participation in Red Flag, according to a pilot who has been flying C-130s "forever," is that it helps erase the image fighter jocks have of MAC "Trash-haulers"—flying civil servants, with the omnipresent plastic spoon in their flight suit pocket for stirring coffee during leisurely cross-country trips. Although, he allows, the fighter pilots don't fraternize much with the MAC aircrews—"except when they come in to the debrief and tell us how many of us they shot down"—there was at least one time when the tables were turned. Here is the legendary "MAC Ace" story:

It happened at Maple Flag a couple of years ago. The C-130 was assigned to the Red force, simulating an AN-12 "Cub," a Soviet short-haul transport similar to the C-130, except for one important difference. Like many Soviet transports, Cubs carry tailguns and C-130s do not. Well—here was their big chance, and the MAC crew wasn't about to pass it up! They went out and got a strobe gun, strapped a loadmaster high in the hold where he could poke the gun out the open upper doors above the ramp at the tail end of the aircraft, took off, and waited for customers.

They didn't have to wait long. In comes the American air hero, taxiing in on the C-130's six o'clock, as so many have done at Red Flag. The fighter calls his shot and then cruises off. Later, at the debriefing, he is showing his gun camera film

C-130 transports from Rhein-Main AFB, Germany, meet up with Myrtle Beach AFB A-10s for refueling and gun loading on dry Texas Lake.

as positive proof that he has bagged yet another whale.

"Wait a minute," says the MAC pilot, barely stifling a giggle. "What are those little flashes coming out from the rear door?"

"Dunno," replied the intrepid fighter jock. "I wondered about that myself."

"Well, I'll tell you what they are. They are 30mm tracer ammunition from our rear guns, and you, Jack, are dead!"

The whole MAC side of the room erupts in guffaws, the cheerful exultation of the triumphant underdogs. It was perhaps MAC's finest hour, and the C-130 crews can't wait for the chance to "Play Red" again.

Not that they get shot down all the time. But the C-130 is a defenseless aircraft and not really built for the mission it performs at Red Flag. MAC pilots have gotten very good at flying the Hercules to the max, scuttling over the ridges and hiding its huge shadow, but they still need help from their fellow Blue fliers in order to survive. Sometimes it's been hard to get the fighter pilots to listen and respond to their needs, but the MAC aircrews say Red Flag is the key to better communication with the TAC jocks.

Sometimes, as in the case of the Strategic Air Command's B-52s, the aircraft aren't part of a mission package at all. The BUFFs—big, ugly, fat fellows, as the B-52s are called—come and go long before the rest of the Players hit the range. They swoop down in cells of three and split up, flying solo over the desert, three minutes and twenty miles apart. The SAC crews aren't anti-social; it's just that the long-range strategic profile they're flying takes too long to plan to be included in the daily Red Flag mission packages, as a Red Flag B-52 officer explains:

The tactical mission starts at eight in the morning. The strategic mission starts two days ahead of time. We're taking off before the people next door have their act together.

Left: Huge B-52Gs taxi at Mather AFB, California, prior to low-level flight through Red Flag exercise. *Above:* B-52s are commonly included in Red Flag scenarios.

The B-52s have been at Red Flag for almost six years now, usually flying more than a dozen sorties a week. The simulated bombing run over the Nellis range is only a small part of their cross-country mission. The huge BUFFs don't land at Nellis, but after they touch down at their bases in California, the crews will sometimes fly back to Nellis in a smaller plane for the debriefing.

The B-52s are always getting "shot down" at Red Flag, but that's no big deal. For one thing, almost all the Red Flag B-52 missions are flown in

B-52 skipper takes huge bird down to 300-feet altitude for single bombing pass through Nellis range.

daytime, but in a war BUFF crews, like Dracula, wouldn't think of venturing out in the daylight. Since most of the shots called on the BUFFs at Red Flag are from visually guided weapons, they have no particular relevance to the B-52's primary mission. Also, BUFF drivers often go looking for trouble, because, as a SAC major explains: "The tailgunners are required to get so much training per quarter, and to get it we'll tell the fighters exactly where the B-52s are going to be, to make sure they do get attacked."

The B-52 flights are just one part of SAC's participation in Red Flag. Almost every other type of aircraft in the SAC inventory has been to Red Flag at one time or another (including the SR-71 Blackbird and the stranger and more spooky electronic

warfare variants of the C-135 series), especially during the annual Rapid Deployment Force and electronic warfare-oriented Red Flags. But perhaps SAC's most important contribution to the Red Flag program has been their tanker support.

SAC's KC-135 tankers have been a regular participant in Red Flag since the beginning. There are usually about five tankers allotted to each Red Flag, although the number can go as high as eight or nine in a Rapid Deployment Force Red Flag. ("There are awesome fuel requirements for certain scenarios that are in plans," says a SAC liaison officer at Nellis.)

Some Red Flag tankers do land at Nellis, but most take off and land at their own bases. Each KC–135 will take on around 155,000 pounds of fuel for each four and a half hour mission. It will use roughly half that, 80 to 85,000 pounds, to refuel about half a dozen aircraft each mission, depending on the type of aircraft and how thirsty it is. (The F–4 is a particularly heavy drinker.) The tanker force takes on about 3 million pounds of fuel for the average two-week Red Flag segment. Since it costs about $25,000 to fill up a KC–135, it's easy to see why fuel is Red Flag's biggest budget item.

At Red Flag the tankers are usually given the call sign "ANKER" and set up tanker tracks for Blue aircraft, orbiting over the Caliente Military Operating Area. The tankers never go east of Student

BUFF crew's view of Nevada desert at 300 feet, 300-plus mph.

Gap, never leave the "no-play" area, and are never attacked. But, like the AWACS and other electronic warfare platforms orbiting out of the ranges, they are sometimes attacked in a simulated way.

"They orbit the AWACS out of the area, because they like to practice long-range stuff," says an Aggressor pilot.

But we'll pick a point between us and AWACS and try to get to that point, and the Eagles will defend. Of course, the AWACS has to recognize the fact that they are being attacked and work their defense.

107

Crew of EF-111A awaits takeoff on crowded Nellis runway. Radome of E-3A AWACS is in background.

"There's only one problem with AWACS," says the Red Flag CO. "It's so good the guys rapidly stop looking around."

How do you solve that problem? Easy; take the AWACS down. But some other USAF electronic warfare platforms are more difficult to work into Red Flag scenarios, because they're also too good. The EF-111A, designed to jam the GCI radar controlling Soviet point-defense fighters like the MiG-21, has already been to Red Flag. It proved two things: one, that it works; and two, it works too well to use in the first few missions. It blinds the GCI controlling the Aggressor's F-5s and gives the Blue side an unfair advantage.

"I want the war to happen," says the Red Flag commander. "So I have to be very careful as to how I use some of these assets, like the EF-111."

Electronic warfare is a big part of Red Flag. Some exercises, such as Green Flag, are devoted almost completely to EW, and for the Blue side it's always the toughest part to master.

"The Soviet's publicized goal is for electronic warfare to take out 30 percent of the opposing forces," says a Red Flag officer. "Thirty percent taken out of the battle without firing a shot."

The most prevalent, and annoying, aspect of electronic warfare at Red Flag is the use of com-jam, blocking out or spoofing the communications among the members of the Blue force. Pilots learn very quickly to make their radio transmissions short and to make sure they know exactly whom

they're talking to; otherwise, they run the risk of being tricked, as the pilots were in this little com-jam fable told by a Nellis range officer:

When the winds get up to fifty knots around here, the visibility goes way down, because you start getting a lot of dust. So when the wind's about thirty-five knots when the guys take off, they [OPFOR EW officers] try to convince them the wind's up to fifty knots now, and there's a weather recall. It's very embarrassing when they come back alone with a full load of bombs and the wind's not blowing near fifty knots.

Is Red Flag's emphasis on com-jam realistic? Here's what an Aggressor, who used to train Jordanian pilots, has to say on the subject:

I was airborne when the first Syrian MiGs were shot down by the Israelis in 1978. I was about

Crew chief of Air National Guard "Green Giant" rescue chopper observes engine start.

120 miles away from the fight. I couldn't talk to my wingman. Com-jamming was quite severe.

Not all the dirty tricks are electronic, however. The bad guys are always up to something at Red Flag.

"There's a lot of cat and mouse in Red Flag," says an Aggressor captain.

Sometimes the mission commander will say, "Okay, guys, all six of us are going to run after A-B-Triple-C [the Airborne Command, Control, and Communications EC–130 that directs the air battle]. We're going to shoot that airplane down!" All the Eagles are thinking, "Well, they'll probably be over by the strikers; no, maybe they'll be over here," and all of a sudden we'll make an end run and get to this guy here. There's a little more gamesmanship in Red Flag, I think, whereas on the road, for us, it's standard Soviet tactics every time.

Another big difference between flying at Red Flag and flying on the road is the fact that we try to integrate an air defense system here, with the ground threats and the air threats. That's the [OPFOR] mission commander's job; maximizing numbers, cycling people in and out, trying to get the most numbers on as many people as we can, integrating the whole force into what they [the Blue Players] might be expected to see. The total concept, as far as air operations is concerned, is more realistic at Red Flag.

Another aspect of Red Flag unusual for the Aggressors is that, as adversary air, they are given help to stop the Blue Force. The help usually comes in the form of Navy or Marine F–4s, although many other types of aircraft have flown on the Red side, including F–15s.

"Occasionally, I'll put Eagles on the other side," says the Red Flag CO.

Well, that changes the nature of the game. They don't have an F–15 yet, so we don't do that on a daily basis. But just to mix it up, we'll throw the whole thing out of balance. What you get is a cold slap in the face. Even though you now think you have the Soviet system figured out, you find that it too can change, that you don't know it all. It's a perspective adjustor. The history of warfare is replete with perspective adjustors.

Usually, however, it's the Navy who fights the Air Force. This too is realistic. The "anchor clankers" are given appropriately nautical call signs— "GULF," "SCALEY," and "SCUBA" are typical examples—and are then unleashed on the Blue forces. The Players given the role of adversary aircraft are not necessarily simulating Soviet tactics. The Aggressors are, of course, but the other Red air heroes are using their own tactics. Navy pilots fly like Navy pilots, which is to say damn good, and much better than your average enemy pilot. If that's unrealistic—too bad. To make them simulate Soviet tactics, which they are not trained to do, wouldn't do them or the pilots they're fighting against any good.

Even though the other adversary aircraft aren't too deeply enmeshed in the highly regimented style of Soviet air defense, the Aggressors welcome the company:

"Red Flag tries to simulate the multi-threat— large numbers of aircraft in a realistic environment," says a 64th AS pilot.

When we go on the road, we usually fly against a particular aircraft and we train them. When we go to Red Flag, we've usually got all the different types of planes in the same semiwar.

Red Flag is good training for us, in that we've got multi-threats against us at the same time we're trying to attack someone else. Our main problem with Red Flag is trying to support it with enough time on station. Numbers and time-wise, it's not all that unrealistic, compared with the aircraft we're emulating. We probably stay on station longer than a MiG–21 would, the difference being they probably wouldn't have so far to drive.

The Aggressor's F–5Es are not air-refuelable, but the other adversary aircraft usually are, so the Red Force sometimes gets their own tanker, orbiting just outside the range. Blue Players sometimes complain that they have to go all the way back to Caliente to rendezvous with their tanker, while OPFOR's is just across the street. But the point of having the Red tanker so close is to give the OPFOR Players longer time on station. After all, in any war, the Air Force expects to find itself in the middle of an overcast of gull-gray Fishbeds, and the Aggressors have a hard enough time keeping even a token adversary fighter force in the air as it is. Not counting the other Players who fly for Adversary Air, the number of Aggressor aircraft assigned to a particular Red Flag mission can be

as high as ten, but the usual number is half a dozen. And to put even that many in the air sometimes takes some doing.

"You've got to realize we've got twelve jets gone on the road between the two squadrons all the time," says an Aggressor pilot.

You've got the periodic maintenance phase inspections, and a certain percentage are flat going to be broke. You have a certain number of airplanes that are allocated to train the Aggressors. So now we're crunching numbers trying to get airplanes to support Red Flag. We're allocated sorties and flying time and gas, just like all the other squadrons. We don't have an unrestricted

Eagle jocks pop cold ones after long ferry flight to Red Flag 82–5.

training capability where we can just take jets and go fly.

To make up for this, the Aggressors have developed a few tricks to maintain a high visibility profile at Red Flag.

"We try to structure our takeoff times so we have the maximum number of airplanes against their maximum numbers at the same time," says a 65th Aggressor jock.

If we have six airplanes to work with, sometimes we'll send two guys out to hit the initial strike force,

111

Above: A-10 pilot firing 30mm gun at ground target.

and then we'll send four more guys out, so that at one time—maybe a ten-minute period—we'll have all six airplanes in the area at one time. The first two will leave early, and then another two-ship will leave, but we'll still keep some people on station to provide a threat.

What the Blue Force doesn't know is when we're going to be there and how many people are going to be there. When they're flying along, working their way in to attack the target, they don't know how many of the Red guys are out there. Even if you have only two Aggressors out there at the time, they don't know that and they're constantly looking for a larger number of threats. The pressure is still on.

Another Aggressor says the important thing at Red Flag is to show the Red Flag:

Our role is to be seen, to attack people, and to be attacked by people and be a threat. So I slow

down and save gas, because it's so far out there and so far back. We can't go out there and race around with our hair on fire at 700-indicated, fifty feet off the ground, and never see anybody, and then run out of gas and come home. So when I'm flying Red Flag, I usually throttle back to 350, 300 sometimes, just kind of cruise along. And when I see somebody, I'll maybe just fly in front of him, and he'll think, "Hey! There goes an F-5!" And then they get real excited, and their airplane shakes up and down.

That usually happens only in the first couple of Red Flag missions, when the Players are constantly surprised by the F-5's small size and smokeless engines, often not getting a Tally-ho (a visual sighting) on the F-5s until they're a mile away. In modern air combat, that's right on your bumper. For example, the F-4's smoking engines and huge size often allow their opponents to get Tallies as far as ten miles away or even farther on good days. (USAF Phantom jocks are constantly amazed—and frustrated—by the Air Force's neglect in modifying the engines in its F-4s to keep them from smoking in military power, as the U.S. Navy, the RAF, the Israeli Air Force, and the Air National Guard have done with their Phantoms.) The F-15 is also a rather large airplane; the span of its horizontal stabilizer is greater than the wingspan of an F-5. Out in the desert, there's no place to hide: no clouds to stash Eagles in, no ground haze or forests where the low-flying, greenery-camouflaged strikers might lose themselves. The Blue Players are not sour grapes—being seen and attacked is part of Red Flag—but they *are* upset when people draw the wrong conclusions about why they were shot down.

"As far as the air-to-air game goes," says an Eagle driver at Red Flag, "if you really wanted to make it realistic, you'd say:

"Okay, Aggressors, you get a hundred aircraft. F-15s, you have fifty aircraft. Now, this is the shot criteria, and when you're killed, you turn around and come back home, and we'll take one away from your big group." Assuming we could get the shot calls passed—and everybody's stuck with that ROE—that would be the only way you could figure out whether you're winning the air-to-air game.

His "enemy," a 64th Aggressor pilot, agrees that Red Flag combat results shouldn't be taken out of context:

A lot of times people will get a slanted view— the Aggressors winning here or not winning there. You set up different ROEs and different mission objectives. For instance, if we're fighting an F-15, he can lock us up on radar and kill us before he even sees us. But they'll often restrict themselves into not shooting before they see the other aircraft

so that we can get into a fight and they can practice their aircraft handling, their BFM [Basic Fighter Maneuvers] and ACT [Air Combat Training].

The Air Force is constantly on guard against people trying to use the results from Red Flag exercises to prove their own bizarre theories about air combat. The USAF learned its lesson from AIMVAL/ACEVAL, a series of tests over the Nellis ACMI range that endeavored to find the best way to employ the new "magic missiles" and wound up with, according to one Nellis officer who was involved with the tests, "enough data to prove anything you wanted to prove." As the real-time data links from the range become more widespread and sophisticated, there will be an even greater tendency for outsiders, particularly contractors and military reformers, to "keep score" at Red Flag.

"Our society has a great desire for numbers," says the Red Flag CO.

But we are trainers and the environment is training, so we have to be careful to keep the guys free to think through the problems that are created out here, to arrive at solutions, as long as they are reasonable.

To the pilots, *why* they were shot down or shot somebody else down is more important than the mere numbers. The idea is not to keep score but to learn from every mission. This is why there are so many briefings at Red Flag. An Aggressor pilot, for example, can go through as many as four briefings for a single flight: a joint briefing with the other members of the adversary air, a preflight briefing with the members of his own flight, a debriefing with his other flight members to make sure they've got their side of the mission straight, and a face-to-face debriefing with the Blue pilots they just flew against.

The Blue Players get at least four briefings as well, and the air-to-air pilots may have to attend one more, the face-to-face with the Aggressors. There are usually two cycles of activity at Red

Flag, one in the morning and one in the evening, called, respectively, the A.M. Go and the P.M. Go. Each mission will have a mass briefing and debriefing, as well as a private brief and debrief among the flight members, usually thirty minutes later. Some of these meetings, especially the mass debriefings, where the pilots have to stand up in front of the rest of the Players and recount what happened during the flight, can be pretty dynamic.

"I don't ever recall a fight," says the Red Flag CO. "Now, I've heard some foul language, but that's hard to discern whether it's in jest or just typical fighter pilot talk."

For whatever reasons, the confessions uttered in the mass debriefings are for the pilots only and are never open to the public.

There is no score at Red Flag, but there are plenty of postgame interviews, and this is where the real value of the program comes in. It may be possible to use the training constraints to rack up a big score. It may even be possible to snow the other pilots into thinking you did better than you did (although don't count on it). But it's impossible to fool yourself, especially when the other pilots— the guys you flew with and the guys you flew against—are sitting around the same table, telling you the way you saw it was not the way it was.

"We're always supposed to check behind us— 'check six,' we call it—because there's always going to be someone sneaking up behind you," says an F–15 pilot at Red Flag.

And you're just kidding yourself if you think, "Well, I'm going so fast no one can catch me." Because, if they were really going to throw missiles out there, you'd get yourself shot down in a day or two. That's like saying, "I do this, and I know it's unsafe, but it's okay." One of the big things is admitting it to yourself. Because, Christ, if you don't admit it to yourself, you're going to kill yourself.

Meanwhile, the war rages on over Redland. Those notional yet nasty Redlanders have taken over the Kawich Valley Industrial Complex (again),

but are about to be pushed back by the Blue Forces (again), and, at the end of the two-week campaign Redland will be vanquished. But Blueland will have to pay the reparations, in the form of more junked trucks, more derelict aircraft, more target-trash to be pounded back into the desert floor by the incoming Blue Forces. But wait—does Blueland ever *lose* the war?

"Yeah, once," says the Red Flag commander.

We got nuked. A couple of exercises ago, I told them, "I'm tired of winning—let's nuke Nellis!" So we got nuked on the last day."

But he cautions against drawing any conclusions from the scenario:

You can't get too many gold watches involved in this. If we have to change the scenario every day, if the FEBA will move a hundred miles tomorrow so that the aircrews have a different set of problems, we'll do that.

The Players understand that the scenario is a function of their capabilities and training requirements, and they don't get too caught up with winning and losing the big war either.

"I'm sure they just want to keep things moving," says an Eagle pilot.

If we're doing really good—and supposedly we're marching the FEBA right up to the northwest corner of the range—shoot, what do you do, call off Red Flag a week early? Say, "Okay, you won, go home?"

The Red Flag intel major who thinks the whole thing up says reality too often interrupts his well-laid plans:

If you look, for example, at Soviet doctrine, they hope to achieve a breakthrough of something like 35 to 50 kilometers in the first day. Within five days, they hope to go approximately 200 to 250 kilometers. Well, if I was to take that and try to superimpose it on what we have here, we'd lose the entire war the first day.

We're working basically with a 50 by 90 kilometer area. So their first day's advance is quite

healthy, because it starts way up off the map. Second day, pretty good. But the third day, although they're still advancing, we can't allow them to advance very far.

The poor Redland premier has his hands full, trying to keep the Russians out of Las Vegas, trying to come up with something worthwhile for each of the Blue Players to do, and, most difficult of all, trying to keep the two worlds, the real and the notional, straight in his mind.

You have to create a story. You make it as plausible as you can, within the constraints. It would serve no real purpose to use real units; it would complicate the exercise process by making the

F-15s are equipped with videotape gun cameras which permit instant viewing for debrief.

whole thing classified, and we'd end up tying our hands when we don't have to. There's some pattern to it. You can't get away from your own knowledge of what's going on in the world; you're not going to have Canada invading Mexico, that type of thing.

You're playing both worlds. You're playing your world and you're playing completely make-believe. I spent the first couple of days here just shaking my head.

Chapter 6
30 Minutes Over Tonopah

0600

Threat Radar Operators: Beatty, Nevada

They're up before the first flight hits the range, and they stay until the last one leaves. They travel more than thirty miles to work, an hour and a half of bone-bruising four-wheel driving over the ridges and razorbacks to the temporary buildings of

Tolicha Peak Electronic Warfare Range. They alternate between freezing and burning on the way to work, and excitement and boredom when they get there. They are the enlisted personnel who operate the radar systems, simulating the electronic threats American pilots would face in another war, and they take their work seriously. They may be stuck four days of the week out in the boondocks, huddled together in contract hotels or rented trailers. The hours are long and the work they do might not make them well liked by pilots. But they are respected. The hardships bring them together. And they are very good at what they do.

0700

Mass Briefing: Building 201, Auditorium

"Enemy forces are having to slow down their southerly push, due to the mountainous terrain. A rift has developed between Red and Stark forces, due to Red's striking unions and consequent inability to wage a full battle. Enemy ground forces are starting to suffer from ammo and food shortages, due to resupply convoy sabotages. Red still continues to have the upper hand, partly due to the takeover of Kawich Valley Industrial Complex. Enemy ground concentrations are as depicted. For further information and exact coordinates, see your individual intelligence representative.

"Red air continues to enjoy superiority, but her losses are mounting. AFFOR's beginning to enjoy some successes, particularly on the air-to-ground missions. The front has moved as depicted, approximately five klicks south of yesterday's fight.

"The time has come for Blue to begin a major counterattack. Yesterday's missions were fragged against important areas, such as the Goldflat Helipad, Kawich Airfield, Sun Valley, and various other targets. So far, the results have been very good, almost all the bombs on the target. With your results from this morning, we hope to start pushing them back.

"You all know your targets. Here's the basic rundown for Mission Package 11–11: You have 76–13/Tolicha Airfield, 76–8/Mount Helen SAM,

and 76–12/Tolicha SAM. Mission Package 11–12: 71–7/Stonewall Airfield, 76–1/Tolicha Industrial Complex, 76–2/Tolicha Railyard, and 76–4/Sun Valley Train. Mission Package 11–13 is Combat Air Patrol.

"Here's a quick and dirty look at your active SAM and AAA. Please notice the large numbers and concentrations. As you know from your flights yesterday, there's a lot of stuff moving around and a lot of stuff not officially identified. Be sure to check with your intel rep about the exact locations of the known threats before you step.

"Adversary air is, as you know, the F–4Ns and the F–5Es simulating Flogger Gs. Major tap points are as shown, but common sense should tell you to keep your eyeballs open at all times."

0730

Eagle Flight: Building 201, Briefing Room 6

They get the big picture at the Mass Briefing, but the pilots have to thrash out the details themselves. There's some give-and-take at the beginning, but as time gets short the flight leader settles arguments with a yawn or stare. Just when it seems they will never get anything settled, the briefing is over, planned to the last detail. Air combat may have come a long way since the Red Baron's time, but pilots still slouch, still grouch, and still talk with their hands.

0830

Adversary Air Brief: 64th Aggressor Squadron Auditorium

It's no secret that Navy admirals and Air Force generals sometimes have their differences. The same is true of majors and lieutenant commanders. The Navy is outnumbered at Red Flag and the naval aviators tend to keep to themselves except for wry comments and occasional incredulity at USAF shot-calls. The Air Force responds by assigning the "squids" silly call signs and making a few sarcastic comments of their own: "They haven't finished copying the slide yet. Wait till their lips stop moving."

0900

Aggressor Briefing: 64th Aggressor Headquarters

The Aggressors have done this sort of thing before. Preflight: "Standard," takeoff: "standard," join-up: "standard," fuel status: "standard," . . .

1000

Eagle Flight: Personal Equipment Room,

The pilots dress for work in silence. Each one has his own routine, his ritual procedure for wiggling into the Nomex armor of the modern knight. The second lieutenants make a big show of it, buckling up the G-suit like Jesse James strapping on his guns, smoothing their hair before screwing on the astronaut style skullcap. The old heads, the majors and lieutenant colonels, dress in silence, unconsciously, with no more wasted motion than Terry Bradshaw suiting up for the Super Bowl.

1030

Eagle Flight: End of Runway Inspection

Los Angeles at rush hour has nothing on the jam-up at the end of the Nellis runways. The home of the fighter pilot is also the birthplace of gridlock. If Red Flag is supposed to teach innovation and improvisation in the air, then pilots get their share of it when their elaborate mission planning melts like snow in the Nevada desert because of late take-off times.

1045

Allah Flight: Stonewall Airfield

Here's Boomer! The BUFF drivers don't tap-dance around the facts. This is a nuclear strike practice mission. Had this been an actual alert, the desert would be glowing by now, and there would be no need for the mission package that follows. The B–52s don't carry live nukes, of course, but they do drill with the SRAAM (Short Range Air-to-Air Missile) simulator; and when that bomb bay opens, just a little bit, you get a creaking feeling in your stomach, too.

122

1100

Weasel Flight: Mount Helen

They *were* an arrow, a twenty-five-ton projectile headed for the heart of Kawich Valley. Now they are low, level, and lurching across the desert floor, saving up energy for the big move ahead. The pilot jerks back on the stick; and behind him the electronic warfare officer feels the Gs dig in as the nose of the big F-4G points up at the sky over Belted Peak.

The Bear struggles to pull his head up close to his scopes. The glare from the sun is tremendous —it's right above them now, washing the cockpit in yellow light. He strains his neck and eyes, peering into the scopes. Suddenly the CRTs flash and sparkle like the Vegas Strip itself, each point of light representing a mortal danger.

Then the screens go blank. The bad guys have recognized the blip on *their* scope for what it is, a threat, and not a target. They've shut down their radars, but it's too late. Their images are frozen in green phosphorescence on the EWO's scopes, the electronic fingerprints already transmitted to the AWACS and on to the rest of the package.

The Weasels hit the floor again, the pair of them arcing like dolphins. They take turns keeping the sites covered. The SAM operators have shut down for good, it seems. The Weasels won't blow anybody up this mission, but if they can keep the missile batteries too frightened to shoot at the strike flight, they will consider it a successful mission.

1105

Baron Control: Range Control Center

"I have one contact just coming down the ridgeline over Pahute Mesa. Looks like he's heading southwest—that should be a Weasel bearing about three-six-zero for six miles from, ah, FITTER, I think.

"I've got a flight of four Eagles over Worthington Peak—looks like they're westbound now.

"Okay, the Eagles are twenty-seven and thirty. I've got somebody just north of FITTER—a Weasel just north of FITTER at about, ah, six thousand feet.

"There's strikers over Coyote at six thousand heading west; I've got Eagles at thirty thousand over Worthington Peak, looks like they're starting to head southwest now—contacts are all on the western part of Pahute Mesa

"FITTER, the only contacts I have in your area are about two-three-zero for ten miles.

"Okay, MIG, the Eagles are zero-three-zero for twenty-two miles southwest bound, pointing at you at thirty thousand feet.

"IVAN, from you estimate the Eagles about zero-three-zero for twenty-two.

"I have a contact on the Eagles now at zero-two-zero from IVAN—no, correction, from me. There's a four-ship wall coming at you twenty-two thousand feet, twenty-two miles."

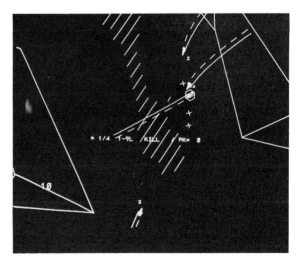

1110

Hazer 01: Pahute Mesa

He's got the pictures, and now he's heading out of the range at 700 knots. At that speed the desert is just a brown blur, the landscape washing around the Phantom's big nose like waves across the prow of his ship; so fast, in fact, that the scene he sees through the canopy bow is actually a picture of what he's *already past*. No one can catch him at this speed, so the pilot relaxes a bit, just long enough to look out the side, where he sees—an F-5! An Aggressor is flying wing on him! The Gomer has ramped down from way above and can't keep up for very long, so he gives the recce bird a little wave, a friendly reminder that no one who thinks he is safe out here ever is.

1120

Eagle Flight: Worthington Peak

Here comes the Wall of Eagles!

The four F-15s are line abreast, about a mile apart, 30,000 feet above the Dinosaur. They're not hiding from anyone. It's impossible to hide an Eagle anyway—Air Force pilots call it the "twin-tailed tennis court." Everyone knows who they are and what they're doing. Spread out across the sky, scanning the range with their powerful radar,

the wall makes it harder for anyone to sneak up behind them. And when they get to the free-fire zone, the areas in the west where the visual ID rules are suspended, they can start throwing Sparrows around, confident that whoever's out there isn't "one of us." (The only other Blue Players out there are the Weasels, much lower and directly beneath them; the B-52s and recce bird having come and gone ten minutes ago, an eternity out on the range.)

But mostly, the wall of Eagles is a scare tactic, a balls maneuver. *Come on out and fight, you Gomer Devils*, it says. *Give us your best shot!*

Of course, it would work best on *real* Gomers, not the Aggressors, who are used to this sort of thing and are not that impressed anymore. Eagle 01 picks up a couple of F-5s on his radar, down low, and a couple a few miles back, higher. The old Kuban shelf again. He begins to lock up on one of the bandits for an AIM-7 shot, and the other one *disappears!* Gone, just like that. Wiped clean off the screen.

This is not the Romulan cloak of invisibility, merely a zero-Doppler turn, the Aggressor's favorite trick. Within a certain range, the F-15's radar can only track the bandit it's locked onto. The other Gomer turns at a right angle to the Eagle, where the radar always has a tougher time following.

Eagle 01 calls a Sparrow shot, waits five seconds, and calls another. The kill is passed. Now where did the other Gomer go?

1125

Ratch Flight: Gold Flat

Up and down, up and down. Fighter pilots don't mind taking positive Gs so much. It's the *negative* Gs, the kind you get on a roller coaster, that are particularly uncomfortable, and nobody pulls more negative Gs than 'Vark drivers.

The terrain-following radar guides them over the jagged ridges; the crew has selected the "hard" ride, full *macho tactical*, and the big plane hawks up and down like a crazy elevator with them in it, rolling like dice in a cup.

But it works. The F–111 uses the terrain-following, along with its extra gas, to hide out in places where the Aggressors would never look, so low the evil electrons from the threat radars whiz over their canopy.

"The F–111s were commended yesterday. Nobody could find us. They thought we were doing touch-and-go's at Indian Springs."

1130

Flogger Flight: Quartzite Mountain

Just cruising along as the second stairstep in the old *Kubanskaya Etazherka*, Flogger 21 is incensed to hear that he has been shot down. He hasn't even seen an Eagle! He hasn't even gotten to the fight yet, and he hears a call passed over the radio: "Fox One kill on the bandit over Quartzite."

He is incensed, but not surprised; this sort of thing happens all the time when they're late taking off, and the Eagles catch them over the free-fire zone. He cranks the F–5 around, and he and his wingman head back to Cedar Pass, their regeneration point. He's mad now, but wait till he finds out the Eagles have capped the regeneration point, too.

1135

Cubby Flight: Kawich Valley

Cubby 52 thought he saw something flashing out on his port wing. He can't worry about that now; he's on final for his pop-up delivery, and live ordnance is a bigger concern than fake MiGs. At the top of his pull-up, he spins the big plane over and heads, upside down, for the desert floor. The target, a fixed SAM site scratched out on the desert floor, has already been pounded by other members of his flight. At the bottom of the dive, Cubby 52 pickles the bombs, lights the burners, and heads out. He won't know until later if he hit the target or not, but he knows right away he's been had; the WSO behind him calls out an F–5 in perfect Atoll parameters. That's the trouble with Eagles—they're never around when you need them.

1600

Mass Debrief: Building 201 Auditorium

So you think you had a good mission? So you think you shacked the target, crumped it, waxed it? Think again. Here you are, on television, starring in the "Optically-guided Threat Hour," where your plane is shown, stuck in the cross hairs of the video camera, shot down by a miserable enlisted man skulking among the rocks *before you dropped your bombs.* How hot is that, ace? Scream if you want, but there's a limit to what the other fighter pilots, your mission peers, will put up with.

In Ivy League colleges, they still have "rank sessions," where a student's "friends" take him apart, piece by piece, tell him everything that may be wrong with him. The idea is to make better people through criticism. And that's what the mass debrief is all about. Did you do well? Great! But more often than not, that means somebody else did poorly. Let's find that poor unfortunate and dump on him —for his own good.

1630

Eagle Flight Debrief:
Briefing Room 6

Back in the security of his own flight, the pilot relaxes a bit. These are, after all, members of his own squadron, his own flight, even his wingman; although they may occasionally have words in private, they present a united front to the rest of the Air Force. The idea here is not to "win the debriefing," but to get their story straight, because soon they'll be "meeting the Aggressors," where the truth will come out if it takes all day—and it often does.

1700

Aggressor Face-to-face:
Building 201

After much debate, after all the pilots' right hands have shot down their left hands and all the cockpit audiotapes have been spooled out into static, the enemies have come to an understanding, a truce. Everybody knows what he did well or did poorly, what he should look out for next time, and what were just the breaks. More than likely, these mortal foes will head for the Nellis Officers Club and still talk about the day's fight, but the main points have been made, and no amount of "aircrew debriefing fluid" will change them.

And what about our young lieutenant, our air-to-air neophyte for whom Red Flag is produced? This is simulated combat mission number seven of a series of ten, and what did he learn about war today?

"I learned a lot of things. Mostly, I've learned it's going to be a real bear to do your job and keep alive."

Typical Order of Battle

Type Aircraft	Call Sign		Mission	Unit	Base
1 RF–4C	SPEED	07	REC	363 TFW	Shaw AFB, SC
1	FAD	27	REC		
1	CESAR	47	REC		
2 F–4G	HAMMER	81/2	DSP	37 TFW	George AFB, CA
	BASHER	05/6	DSP		
2	BLADE	25/6	DSP		
2	LANCE	05/6	DSP		
2 F–16A	COWBOY	03/4	OCA	474 TFW	Nellis AFB, NV
4	GAMBLER	11/14	OCA		
2 F–15C	FAZER	71/2	CAP	49 TFW	Holloman AFB, NM
2	BARKY	63/4	CAP		
2	HUD	61/2	CAP		
2	SCANT	61/2	CAP		
2	CYLON	71/2	CAP		
2 F–4E	PECOS	21/2	INT	4TFW	Seymour Johnson AFB, NC
2	HYDRA	51/2	BAI		
2	CHOCO	21/2	BAI		
2 F–4E	ARCO	41/2	INT	374 TFW	Moody AFB, GA
2	BEATER	51/2	OCA		
2 F–4C	SATAN	11/2	OCA	184 TFG	Lincoln MAP, NE
2 F–4D	LYNX	41/44	OCA	484 TFW	Homestead AFB, FL
2	SINNER	41/42	OCA		
3 F–111F	RATCH	31/33	INT	48 TFW	RAF Lakenheath, UK
1 RF–4C	DERAY	17	REC	26 TRW	Zweibrucken AB, WG
1	HARLY	37	REC		
1 E–3A	EDGY	71	AWC	552 AWACW	Tinker AFB, OK

Typical Order of Battle

Type Aircraft	Call Sign		Mission	Unit	Base
5 KC–135	ANKER	10/20/ 30/40/ 50	AAR	207 AREFG	Travis AFB, CA
2 F–5	MIG	11/2	ADF	57 FWW	Nellis AFB, NV
2	IVAN	21/2			
2	FITTER	31/2			
2	BARON	11/2			
2	FLOGGER	2/2			
2	DAGGER	31/2			
2 F–4N	SCUBA	41/42	ADF	VF–202	NAS Dallas, TX
2	SCALY	51/52	ADF		
2	GULF	61/62	ADF		

Aggressor Camouflage Schemes

This is a listing of the 22 F-5Es assigned to the 64th Aggressor Squadron at Nellis AFB, summer 1982. The aircraft numbers are the last two (or sometimes three) numbers of the aircraft's serial number, stenciled in large "buzz numbers" on either side of the aircraft's nose. "Camo" is the nickname given to the paint scheme by the Aggressor pilots—camouflage finishes throughout the Aggressor community are similar, although they might have different nicknames.

Number	Camo	Number	Camo
847	Pumpkin	539	Gray
865	Banana	541	Ghost
882	Sand	557	Blue
508	Ghost	558	Lizard
511	Silver	564	Snake
514	Ghost	567	Sand
515	Ghost	568	Snake
519	Ghost	570	Blue
528	Gray	635	Gomer
531	Blue	636	Silver Gray
537	Gray	396	Blue

George Hall

The Author

Former writer and editor for the *St. Petersburg Times* and the *Washington Star*, Michael Skinner is currently on the staff of Cable News Network in Atlanta, Georgia. He is author of *USAFE: A Primer of Modern Air Combat in Europe* (Presidio Press, 1982).

James A. Sugar

The Photographer

George Hall is a San Francisco photographer specializing in aerial and aviation topics. He is co-author of *The Blimp Book* (Squarebooks), *Working Fire: The San Francisco Fire Department* (Squarebooks), and *The Great American Convertible* (Doubleday). His photos illustrated the 1980 book *CV: Carrier Aviation* (Presidio Press) and *USAFE: A Primer of Modern Air Combat in Europe* (Presidio Press, 1982).

Other books in the Presidio AIRPOWER Series:

USAFE: A PRIMER OF MODERN AIR COMBAT IN EUROPE
Michael Skinner
Photography by George Hall

$9.95   ISBN-0-89141-151-8

CV: CARRIER AVIATION
Peter Garrison
Photography by George Hall

$9.95   ISBN: 0-89141-074-0

SAC: A PRIMER OF MODERN STRATEGIC AIRPOWER
Bill Yenne

Fall 1984   ISBN-0-89141-189-5

MARINE CORPS AIR: "SEMPER FI"
John Trotti
Photography by George Hall

Spring 1985   ISBN-0-89141-190-9